UNFORBIDDEN PLEASURES

UNFORBIDDEN PLEASURES

Adam Phillips

HAMISH HAMILTON
an imprint of
PENGUIN BOOKS

HAMISH HAMILTON

UK | USA | Canada | Ireland | Australia
India | New Zealand | South Africa

Hamish Hamilton is part of the Penguin Random House group of companies
whose addresses can be found at global.penguinrandomhouse.com.

Penguin
Random House
UK

First published 2015
001

Set in 12.5/16 pt Fournier MT Std
Typeset by Jouve (UK), Milton Keynes
Printed in Great Britain by Clays Ltd, St Ives plc

A CIP catalogue record for this book is available from the British Library

ISBN: 978-0-241-14579-1

www.greenpenguin.co.uk

For Judith

— to define — is to distrust.

Laurence Sterne, *The Life and Opinions of Tristram Shandy*

This has caused me the greatest trouble and still does always cause me the greatest trouble: to realize that what things are called is unspeakably more important than what they are.

Friedrich Nietzsche, *The Gay Science*

I suffered
A terrible hangover
Of faith.

Olena Kalytiak Davis, 'It Was a Coffin That Sang'

A child always, in part, wants even to be weaned.

Edna O'Shaughnessy, 'The Absent Object'

Contents

Laying Down the Law

We seem never to ask 'Why do you know?' or 'How do you believe?'

J. L. Austin, 'Other Minds'

I

When Oscar Wilde famously said that the problem with socialism was that it took up too many evenings, he was reminding us that there may always be things we care about more than the things we care about most; and that, however much we care about something, there are always other things that we want to do. That, inevitably, there is something forbidding about socialism; it may want us to give up too much. Just like any of our commitments there is much that it excludes, and much that it rejects. Whatever we permit ourselves we are forbidding ourselves something else. All our ideals for ourselves – all our aims and aspirations and beliefs – are by definition restrictive. And that is their point and their purpose. But for Wilde, in this all too ordinary fact – we can't do everything, believe everything, love and desire everyone – there is a troubling and absurd selective inattention. We may be a little too keen to make the necessary sacrifices; we may relish giving things up. Indeed, we may do what we do because of what we have to give up in order to do it.

Something is made possible – or so it seems, Wilde intimated – by making many other things impossible; or even unthinkable, inconceivable. And yet we are strangely haunted by some of the things and people we are persuaded to exclude. To forbid something is to make it unforgettable (children must not cross the road without looking; adults must not think too much about sex, or the wrong kind of sex). At its best and at its worst to forbid is to coerce attention and to guarantee interest. It is to arrange a haunting. We must always be mindful, somewhere in ourselves, of what we have been forbidden, of what we have forbidden ourselves; being out of control is the way we tend to describe our doing of these forbidden things; though it does not follow that when we do unforbidden things we are in control. It is, in fact, only because we have created forbidden things that we have created the idea of being in control. Our ideas and experiences of pleasure have been muddled by being associated with control. So when we speak of unforbidden pleasures, we should note, we no longer need the language of control, of discipline and punishment. We can forget about those particular words. This is what Wilde was referring to when he wrote, in 'The Critic as Artist' (1891), 'We teach people how to remember, we never teach them how to grow.' We may not be able to teach people *how* to grow, but in order to grow there are things you need to be able to forget.

It is, of course, Wilde's point that socialism interferes with sociability. And that, by implication, we can use commitment, conviction, strong belief – and, Wilde will assert, morals and purposes – to narrow our minds (and stunt our growth). As though there is always a temptation, or a desire, to forget the multifariousness of our pleasures; to simplify (and sanitize) our hedonism in the service of traditional safeties; the forgetting of pleasures being one form that the renunciation of pleasure can take (the one formalized by psychoanalysis). As though we are always laying down the law for ourselves, and the law forces our attention (tells us what we should and shouldn't be looking at, who we should and shouldn't be listening to). We are taught to remember everything except our pleasures, Wilde implied. And this is where art comes in: 'All art is immoral,' Wilde said, and so it is in art that we recover our real pleasures; we recover everything morality forces us to renounce. What Wilde called 'recognising no position as final' means not taking the forbidders too seriously; that is, not taking them on their own terms. Significant changes in manners and morals – periods of significant change in personal and cultural history – always involve the re-description of previously forbidden desires. One way or another the forbidden becomes the less forbidden, or even the unforbidden, and so provides a different kind of pleasure (we are released into enjoying previously forbidden things in different ways: released into what Kathleen Stewart calls, in *Ordinary Affects*, a new 'tangle of potential connections'). And some forbidden pleasures remain just that, forbidden, because our lives would be intolerable otherwise. But we should, Wilde suggested, seek out the immoral in order to see what we think and feel about it, and this is where art comes in. We need to be able to think and talk about where our real enjoyment is, and why it might be where it is. We need to find out whether we can replace what we *should* enjoy with what we *do* enjoy.

Wilde wondered why we were so impressed by, so serious about, forbidden pleasures; why, that is to say, we might want to be intimidated by morality and tantalized by pleasure, and to so relish suffering the consequences of our renunciations. If we could believe, if we could live as if, as he put it, 'Aesthetics are higher than ethics . . . Even a colour-sense is more important, in the development of the individual, than a sense of right and wrong,' he believed our lives would be better. We might, for example, be able to enjoy living in a world of unpredictable consequences, or of what Bernard Williams calls 'moral luck', if we preferred aesthetics to ethics. Ethics is prophetic, Wilde implied, in a way that aesthetics need not be; it is prescriptive, it aspires to determine causes and consequences. It attempts to predict the future. By telling us what our lives *should* be like, morality often claims to be telling us what our lives are *really* like (even though we are often left feeling that we are failing to live our lives as they really are). What would our lives be like, Wilde's heroes want us to imagine, if we found the forbidden a little less forbidding; if we used the idea of forbidden pleasure to think *with*, rather than to stop our selves thinking (or talking)? Perhaps the whole idea of forbidden pleasure brings out the worst in us. What could our lives be like if we took seriously what Walter Pater – Wilde's erstwhile aesthetic hero – wrote in his 1866 essay on Coleridge: 'Hard and abstract moralities are yielding to a more exact estimate of the subtlety and complexity of our life.' The implication being that the subtlety and complexity of our (modern) lives are not suited to hard and abstract moralities.

What became known as the Aesthetic Movement in England in the later nineteenth century – broadly speaking, the work of Pater and Wilde and their rewriting of the work of John Ruskin, John Henry Newman and Matthew Arnold and the romanticism that preceded them – we can see now as, among other things, an attempt to change an inherited vocabulary; of finding a new way of describing what we are doing and not doing by following a rule (as though we might decide what we want to inherit, and what we want to do with our inheritance: in this case the inheritance of moral vocabularies, of rules and manners, and the forms of life they intend for us, as they speak on our behalf). 'The Aesthetic Movement,' David DeLaura wrote in *Hebrew and Hellene in Victorian England*, was 'a serious and respectable attempt to provide fullness of life to a society increasingly aware, as Arnold put it, that the immense inherited "system of institutions, established facts, accredited dogmas, customs, rules," fails to correspond to the wants of modern life.' An attempt by these late Victorians, as Arnold was to put it in his essay 'Democracy', 'to gain a more vivid sense of their own life and activity.' If, instead of the words 'good' or 'right' (or 'sacred') we use the words 'beautiful' or 'pleasurable' or 'enlivening' – though not, for Wilde, the other late-nineteenth-century candidates 'useful' or 'profitable' – how would our lives be

different? Once the power of redescription is acknowledged, words like 'true', 'good', 'right', 'sacred' – and, of
course, 'forbidden' – are among the first casualties. You
change the conventional absolutes by changing the con-
ventions. Another way of saying this – a less earnest, more
casually pragmatic, way – is: forget certain words and use
less familiar ones instead, and see what happens. If, as
Pater wrote, habit is a form of failure, we should try out
new habits, different ways of speaking.

II

'We are punished for our refusals,' Lord Henry Wotton says
in Wilde's *The Picture of Dorian Gray* (1891); 'Every impulse
that we strive to strangle broods in the mind, and poisons
us . . . The only way to get rid of a temptation is to yield
to it. The glancing allusion to William Blake's *The Marriage of Heaven and Hell* (1790) is deliberate, Wilde being
a keen reader of Blake: 'He who desires but acts not, breeds
pestilence.' In these familiar reversals of Wilde's – 'We are
punished for our refusals'; 'the only way to get rid of a
temptation is to yield to it' – we are being shown language
as an area of freedom, and this freedom as a certain kind
of amusement. We have been bewitched not by a picture

but by a way of putting things; by certain words in a certain order. Particular ways of performing our language have held us captive (habit can be a great deadener of pleasures, forbidden and otherwise). The language that formulates the forbidden can reformulate it: 'A Truth in art,' Wilde wrote in 'The Truth of Masks' (1891), 'is that whose contradictory is also true.' Once we start having it both ways we can see how many ways there may be. This is what Wilde wants to impress upon us. We have taken as orders things better heard as suggestions; we have sought information when we might have preferred evocation, or wanted facts when impressions may have been more conducive. Any given vocabulary is a secret and not so secret moralizer of experience, at once a curse and a blessing, a form of instruction. 'Wilde,' his biographer Richard Ellmann writes, 'was a moralist, in a school where Blake, Nietzsche, and even Freud were his fellows. The object of life is not to simplify it. As our conflicting impulses coincide, as our repressed feelings vie with our expressed ones, as our solid views disclose unexpected striations, we are all secret dramatists.' Even Ellmann, perhaps unsurprisingly, has recourse to what, for Wilde, was the old vocabulary: Wilde, he says, was a moralist (Ellmann uses Wilde's 'Aesthetics are higher than ethics' as the epigraph to his chapter on Dorian Gray). But the tradition that Ellmann creates for

8

Wilde – and in this he was preceded by Harold Bloom – is instructive. We could construe each of these very different writers, from very different cultural traditions, as saying: laying down the law, any law, is stranger and crueller than it looks; the forbidden is always a provocation, whatever else it is; and therefore we should forget certain words and try to remember other ones instead. Extricate yourself, in so far as you can, from the vocabulary that doesn't suit you, that doesn't get you the life you want. Think of the languages you prefer; think of language as a pleasure and not a penance, as a celebration and not a sacrifice. Each of these writers has their key words, their own distinctive idiom, a vocabulary by which we recognize them; and each of these writers, not incidentally, had distinctive things to say about memory; about the useful, the purposeful, the pleasurable forgetting of words.

We want to narrow our minds – we want to speak and write in particular ways – because we want to set limits to our wanting, to our sense of possibility. So it is not incidental that when Wilde came to actually write about socialism, say, in 'The Soul of Man under Socialism' (1891), he writes about many other things as well, and mostly about Art and Individualism – about Art *as* Individualism – and about pleasure as the point of the Art and the Individualism that he capitalizes, and capitalizes on, in this extraordinary essay ('Socialism,' Wilde remarked in conversation, 'is enjoyment'). When he writes about socialism he wants to write about what he takes it that the socialists of his day were in danger of forgetting, and what indeed they should forget about. Intimating that the socialists of his day, in their ideological fervour, had misunderstood what kind of sociability socialism might, or could, entail. Or what kinds of things people might really enjoy doing together. 'The chief advantage that would result from the establishment of Socialism is,' Wilde begins his essay,

> undoubtedly, the fact that Socialism would relieve us from that sordid necessity of living for others which, in the present condition of things, presses so hardly upon almost everybody. In fact, scarcely anyone at all escapes.

Living *for* others is not the same as living *with* others; indeed, living for others, Wilde suggested, might sabotage pleasurable coexistence. Wilde as a classicist would know that 'sordid' – in 'that sordid necessity of living for others' – came from the Latin *sordidus*, 'dirty', and was associated with filth and waste matter. A sordid necessity is then at once wasteful and contaminating. Living for others, which 'scarcely anyone at all escapes', means for Wilde a range of things, from the Christian ethic of self-sacrifice, through the altruism of utilitarianism (doing whatever is conducive to the greatest happiness of the greatest number), to the more modern-sounding notion of simply being what others want us to be; these others to whom we wish to conform being specific and significant, and to some extent chosen (Nietzsche, another critic of Christian altruism, wrote in *Thus Spoke Zarathustra* (1883), 'Please unlearn this "for", you creators: it is precisely your virtue that you shall do no thing for'). The phrase 'living for others' suggests that we can live on behalf of other people's desires, or that we can live in their place or in place of them, or for their benefit, or for their very survival. That we can, as it were, forget ourselves in order to remember them, those others for whom we are living. As though every life was a sacrifice to both the previous generation and to our contemporaries in some infinite regress of obligation and indebtedness (Freud, of course, would write in *Civilization and Its Discontents* (1930) of societies as profoundly and necessarily compromising for the individual and her desire). 'Living for others', with its myriad associations and connotations, is, we might say, integral to the moral vocabulary Wilde inherited; what do these others that we are living for forbid, and encourage? Which others are we living for, and why? If we are not living for others, what or who are we living for? Why does living involve living for? What is it about life – the then modern life – that required justification, or reasons, or foundations, or endorsements? Is it possible that we might begin to believe that there is nothing or no one to live for? And how, if at all, would we live then? These are the kinds of questions that certain ways of using the inherited vocabulary might dissuade us from asking (and that Blake, Nietzsche, Freud, Wilde and many others were asking). What have we got to do with other people? And what do we really enjoy doing with them?

In Wilde's pagan socialism no one would be compliant or servile or modest. They would be, in the very best sense, self-centred, there being no other real centre from which they could live ('For out of ourselves we can never pass,' Wilde wrote in 'The Critic as Artist', 'nor can there be in creation what in the creator was not'; the creator and creation here secularizing and parodying what Wilde took to be the increasingly outworn vocabulary of Christianity: Christianity being a language – despite, or because of, his youthful flirtation with Catholicism – he found it intermittently more difficult to speak with conviction). In Wilde's socialism the artist is exemplary, and exemplary in his disregard of what others want from him. One thing the others want from him being a certain way of talking and writing. What Wilde often referred to as 'Public Opinion' in 'The Soul of Man under Socialism' is always laying down the law; public opinion being defined by Wilde as, 'an attempt to organize the ignorance of the community, and to elevate it to the dignity of physical force'. It is the being forcefully organized that Wilde resents as much as the ignorance cultivated. 'Whenever a community or a powerful section of a community, or a government of any kind, attempts to dictate to the artist what he is to do,' he wrote,

Art either entirely vanishes, or becomes stereotyped, or degenerates into a low and ignoble form of craft. A work of art is the unique result of a unique temperament. Its beauty comes from the fact that the author is what he is. It has nothing to do with the fact that other people want what they want. Indeed, the moment that an artist takes notice of what other people want, and tries to supply the demand, he ceases to be an artist, and becomes a dull or an amusing craftsman, an honest or a dishonest tradesman. He has no further claim to be considered as an artist. Art is the most intense mode of Individualism that the world has known. I am inclined to say that it is the only real mode of Individualism that the world has known . . . alone, without any reference to his neighbours, without any interference, the artist can fashion a beautiful thing; and if he does not do it solely for his own pleasure, he is not an artist at all.

This, of course, is not a fashionable view, at least not in universities, nor among socialists. It was a view, paradoxically, that would ultimately be exploited by a voracious art market. But what I am interested in here, both historically and psychologically, is what Wilde took to be the preconditions for both Art and Individualism: turning a blind eye to other people and what they want (in his wonderful poem 'The Notebooks of Robinson Crusoe', Ian Crichton Smith writes, 'Language is other people'). Wilde's artist does not ask the contemporary question, 'How can I make myself worth investing in?', but asks instead, 'What do I really want to make?' As Wilde put it further on in 'The Soul of Man under Socialism', 'A true artist takes no notice whatever of the public. The public to him are non-existent . . .'; he makes art 'for his own pleasure, and has never asked the public what they wanted, has never cared to know what they wanted'. Wilde is so insistent, we might presume or conjecture, partly because he was all too aware of his own all too compromising desire to please; and of the predations of the market that were commodifying art at an unprecedented rate. The artist, for Wilde, becomes that strange, improbable creature, a law unto himself, supposedly untrammelled by the laws of others. People start to have fantasies about more private languages when the public languages don't do the trick. People start idealizing outlaws when the law is felt to be unduly excluding. The desire for freedom is the desire for new rules. And new rules mean new names for things.

The kind of pleasure, the kind of language, Wilde is wanting and promoting is sabotaged by being or doing what other people want from him (and often, for Wilde, by being encouraged to do rather than just to be). The whole notion of the forbidden, of course, prescribes the individual's legitimate pleasures. And organizes what people can legitimately want from each other (what people are wanting from, and for, each other being the way in which 'the problem' is always formulated). Indeed, what other people might want from the artist, Wilde suggests, destroys him as an artist; his art 'has nothing to do with the fact that other people want what they want'. It is the Art that 'vanishes', that 'degenerates' once the artist starts attending to other people's wants, once he abrogates what Wilde called in 'The Decay of Lying' (1891), 'that healthy natural vanity which is the secret of existence'. Whether it is called the mother or the market, Mama or Mammon, what other people want, at least from the artist, is the saboteur of art and growth. When Ernest suggests, in the dialogue that

is 'The Critic as Artist', that 'great artists work unconsciously [and] that they were "wiser than they knew" ', his
friend Gilbert, the more overtly 'Wildean' character of the
two, replies, 'It is really not so, Ernest. All fine imaginative work is self-conscious and deliberate. No poet sings
because he must sing . . . A great poet sings because he
chooses to sing.' The great artist is self-conscious and deliberate; but in this story the artist can be conscious of himself
only by forgetting the existence of other people (the public, to the Wildean artist, are 'non-existent'). Other people,
in other words, distract us from our selves; what they want
from us – and other people are relentless wanters for
Wilde, monstrous in their greed, and in their greed for
reassurance – distorts and pre-empts what the artist wants
from and for himself. In this purity-and-danger version of
art and individualism, the artist is always endangered by
other people. He is in danger of forgetting himself; and
endangered by the kind of pleasure – the masochistic
pleasure – compliance can bring. To avert this catastrophe
he must forget about other people. He must live as if –
implausible as it might sound – other people, particularly
the arbiters of taste, do not exist. It is, though, a version of
what every child has to be able to do when necessary –
pretend he has no parents, or pretend that his parents are
not really his parents: the child choosing his future by

choosing his inheritance; the child at once wanting to be what the parents apparently need him to be – wanting to restore the parents to their lost perfection – and doing something else entirely. The child as double agent.

III

We can see Wilde as, among other things, trying to find ways of recovering people's pleasure in each other's company (his plays make us enjoy people talking to each other, for example, in quite new ways; as though it was a terrible thing to make talking uninteresting). Something about a certain fantasy concerning the individual and individualism, about what was deemed to be valuable regarding the self and sociability, was felt to be under threat by Wilde, and many of his late-nineteenth-century contemporaries. Indeed, in 1859, the year Darwin published *On the Origin of Species*, John Stuart Mill had written, in what became the manifesto of modern liberalism, *On Liberty*, in a chapter entitled 'Of Individuality', 'He who lets the world, or his own portion of it, choose his plan of life for him, has no need of any other faculty than the ape-like one of imitation.' Mill's *On Liberty* – in which 'the tyranny of the majority', a newly monstrous 'public opinion', threatened to stifle what he called 'The only freedom which deserves the name . . . pursuing our own good in our own way' – was the importantly earnest precursor of Wilde's rather more alluringly stylish preoccupations.

So we might ask, more simplistically, what was the problem that Wilde's particular version of aestheticism was a solution to? Was it the precariousness of the modern individual finding out, and holding on to, what matters most to him? Or the difficulty of living in a world in which collaboration is assumed to be unavailable or unavailing? Or the fear, perhaps, that there may be nothing that matters most, or much, or even enough? Or is it that the whole project of wanting to be a law unto oneself exposes one's fear of other people and how powerful they can be, or seem to be? Indeed, one's morality could turn into no more and no less than one's defiance of other people's moralities. Or it could turn into a new-found moral inventiveness; not merely, as Blake proposed, by the inventing of one's own system to avoid being oppressed by another man's, but also by the finding of new, unoppressive moralities: moralities that are not systems; moralities that could be objects of desire more akin to sexual or aesthetic objects; moralities that could be both relished and exhilarating; moralities that might inspire rather than humiliate. Moralities that might make what people want from each other pleasurable rather than punishing; and might, indeed, change what people want from each other.

This desire for different moralities could make one want to change the game by changing the language game; by finding new things to value, and new kinds of evaluation (and new things to say about evaluation). And all of this would sustain the possibility that both Wilde and Nietzsche refer to: the possibility that one could love being alive. The issue for them was not the difficulty of living, but the difficulty of really enjoying living. They both suggest, in their different ways, that we have been misinformed about our real pleasures (if authorities are people who tell us what we should enjoy, we have to wonder what it might mean to be encouraged to enjoy something). Will developing a colour-sense, Wilde asks, keep you going better than a sense of right and wrong (a version of the question: what are the difficulties involved in changing one's vocabulary, and changing one's vocabulary such that it really changes one's life?)? In his account of the artist, and of the critic as artist, of the artist as the exemplary individual, Wilde is attempting to sustain the idea of the individual through art; as though art were the ultimate proof, or guarantor, of the existence of the individual, and his greatest pleasure. As though individualism, or the pleasure of individualism, was now in doubt, might in fact go under, or even disappear. And the artist was the only person – or represented the only person – who could withstand the intimidation of consensus; who could resist being deformed by opinions and money (what Wilde referred to as the 'vulgar', the 'common'). What we have to be wary of now, he suggests, is having too much in common with other people, and indeed with ourselves. We must be wary of being too knowing about knowingness.

Art, for Wilde, was by definition not rational, because so-called rationality was a species of conformism. 'There are two ways of disliking art,' Gilbert says in 'The Critic as Artist'; 'One is to dislike it. The other, to like it rationally. For Art, as Plato saw, and not without regret, creates in listener and spectator a form of divine madness. It does not spring from inspiration, but it makes others inspired. Reason is not the faculty to which it appeals.' So art drives us mad. Or rather, art helps us to be as mad as we need to be to feel fully alive. Art wants to dispel rationality, the rationality that estranges people from their inspiration. So only bad art in his view can be understood or explained. And this in itself, of course, redescribes the critic's project; the critic in Wilde's account is both akin to the artist and in many ways even superior to the artist – 'criticism is more creative than creation'. The critic is freer to make more of the artist's art than the artist himself is capable of doing. In this account the Wildean critic takes the work of art further than the artist is able to do (explanation and understanding being the enemy of this process, the enemy of the artist's real project). 'The critic,' Gilbert says, is 'in his own way as creative as the artist, whose work, indeed, may be merely of value in so far as it gives to the critic a suggestion for some new mood of thought and feeling which he can realise with equal, or perhaps greater, distinction of form, and, through the use of a fresh medium of expression, make differently beautiful and more perfect.' The art is a pretext for the critic's artistry. The critic creates new evocations in response to the artwork; the criticism itself then becoming a work of art in its turn. But, for the Wildean critic, it needs to be stressed that explaining and understanding a work of art is to miss the point. A real work of art should be strangely affecting; and it need not be in any way informative. John Ashbery's remark that 'the worse your art is, the easier it is to talk about' refers us back to Wilde's 'The Critic as Artist'.

Great art, in Wilde's view – and Wilde always explicitly privileges the literary arts – enables us to forget ourselves, our rational, conforming, intelligible, law-abiding, too timid, explaining selves. And this forgetting makes other things possible. But the artist, we should note, in Wilde's view, neither loses himself nor forgets himself – art 'does not spring from inspiration': the artist is 'self-conscious and deliberate' – he just needs to forget about other people. Wilde's artist is in this sense both conscious and self-conscious, without at least wanting to be merely a propagandist (though of course the Wildean hero is always, paradoxically, too knowing, even though it is often his knowingness that undoes him: Dorian Gray kills himself; Lord Henry Wotton does not). So mindful is Wilde of the power of language that he seeks to use it with deliberation and calculation in the full knowledge that language is virtually defined by its unintended consequences.

The 'influence' – to use one of Wilde's key words – of language is inexplicable but decisive; Wilde wrote, for example, in *The Portrait of Mr W. H.* (1889) that the *Symposium* is Plato's most 'perfect' because the most 'poetical' of the dialogues, which 'began to exercise a strange influence over men, and to colour their words and thoughts, and manner of living'. By colouring people's 'words and thoughts, and manner of living', Plato's words (in Marsilio Ficino's translation) developed people's colour-sense. But though Wilde tries to tell us what the effect was, the word 'strange' in 'strange influence' by definition keeps his options open and unfamiliar ('strange' was another of Wilde's key words, as it was for his erstwhile idol Pater).

'Strange' meaning 'foreign', 'alien', 'uncanny'; as though language estranges us in its very familiarity.

There was propaganda and there were enigmatic objects. Wilde, one could say, in his paradoxical way, was always propagandizing for the enigmatic object, the supreme enigmatic object being language itself, and its strange influence; with the (albeit contentious) implication that if we were to treat morality as an enigmatic object, and not as propaganda, our lives – not to mention our conversations about morality – would be more satisfying. We would be more genuinely puzzled about what we are using morality to do, and about what kinds of pleasure our different moralities might involve us in. And also more intrigued about what kinds of pleasure our different languages make possible. Wilde's 'rhetoric', the critic Linda Dowling writes in *Language and Decadence in the Victorian Fin de Siecle*, 'describes the autonomous life of literary language, hinting at the dangerous effects that such language can have on human life and consciousness'. The danger she describes is of course directed at conventional morality. This dangerous 'autonomous life of literary language' makes the language itself sound like an outlaw, and these 'dangerous effects' of 'such language' that Dowling refers to were to be fateful for Wilde himself.

What kind of 'moralist', to use Ellmann's word, was

Wilde? What kind of moralist can anyone be once they acknowledge, or even want to celebrate, the unintended consequences of language, the strange influence of certain people's words? Or even language itself as a potential outlaw? And if they prefer the aesthetic to ethics, beauty to morality, and so are seeking ways to live aside from the law, or beyond good and evil? The whole idea of the forbidden, of course, gives us an apparently coherent set of causes and consequences – of parameters – by giving us a set of rules and prohibitions, all of which need to be sufficiently understandable to guarantee our obedience. The language of prohibition is the dream of a language of straightforward influence, not strange influence; a language of orders, not impressions. A language of rules, not suggestions. Language as effective propaganda. And yet, of course, as Wilde would reveal again and again – would indeed relish exposing – to forbid something is to make it desirable. The forbidden coerces desire. It makes something strangely alluring. It may make us obedient, but it also makes us dream (often at the same time). To abide by a rule you have to have in mind what it would be to break it.

'It is always,' Wilde wrote in 'The Decay of Lying', 'the unreadable that occurs.' Not, that is, what we have supposedly understood. Whether or not this is strictly true, it reminds us of the pleasures of an amused scepticism. There may be lots of reasons why something is unreadable, but to be unreadable someone must have tried to read it first. Language has its effect, its strange influence, Wilde intimates, even when we are unable to read it. The rules – and especially in their most absolute form as the forbidden, the taboo – have to be readable and unforgettable, accessible and memorable. We have to be able to know what the rules are, and to think of this knowing as, in part, an understanding of what we do with them. We want, depending on our prejudices and preferences, some of the readable to occur, and some of it not to. And, Wilde adds, 'It is always the unreadable that occurs.' What we don't know, what we haven't understood, can be the realest thing about us. It can be what happens.

So I want to read Wilde as encouraging us to forget, or to unlearn, certain words and phrases; to forget a vocabulary – words like 'seriousness', 'duty', 'explanation', 'fact' and 'imitation', and phrases like 'living for others', and 'making oneself useful' ('The sure way of knowing nothing about life,' Wilde wrote, 'is to try to make oneself useful') – and to use words like 'beauty', 'disobedience', 'development', 'pleasure' and 'perfection', and phrases like 'the beauty of life' and 'the joy of living' instead. To forget (or to unlearn) a vocabulary is to foster a remembering of a different self – the enigmatic self, the only self we are ever going to have, if we want to have a self – and its plenitudes and pleasures ('the have-nots and the yearning ones . . . have formed linguistic usage', Nietzsche remarks in 1887 in *The Gay Science*). It is to a celebration of so-called selfishness – his own redescription of 'selfishness' – that Wilde invites us; to the laying down of a different kind of law.

IV

'A man is called selfish,' Wilde said in 'The Soul of Man under Socialism',

> if he lives in the manner that seems to him most suitable for the full realisation of his own personality; if, in fact, the primary aim of his life is self-development . . . Self-ishness is not living as one wishes to live, it is asking others to live as one wishes to live. And unselfishness is letting other people's lives alone, not interfering with them. Selfishness always aims at creating around it an absolute uniformity of type. Unselfishness recognizes infinite variety of type as a delightful thing . . . enjoys it. It is not selfish to think for oneself. A man who does not think for himself does not think at all. It is grossly selfish

to require of one's neighbour that he should think in the same way, and hold the same opinions.

'Infinite variety of type' is a paradoxical phrase, acknowledging that, though there may be types, there may at least be an infinite variety of them. In describing the primary aim of life as self-development – or growth, as he sometimes calls it – Wilde is incorporating ideas from nineteenth-century biology and Darwinism into his aestheticism. And by describing it as 'grossly selfish' to require one's neighbour to think as one does oneself, he is giving a commentary on Christ's injunction to love thy neighbour as thyself; which could also be described as grossly selfish. In all these Wildean stipulations, no one imposes anything on anyone else: it is that virtually unthinkable thing, a morality without intimidation, that Wilde is wanting to conjure up. He is wary, above all, of collusion, of the simulation of shared worlds through intimidation. For Wilde, it is as though the then modern individual was being forced to forget that he might have his own thoughts, his own desires, his own development. As though the pressures of uniformity were becoming unbearable (in Nietzsche's language the instinct for life was being replaced by 'the herd instinct'). What was needed was a redescription, a rewording of selfishness; and so, by definition, of whatever the self was deemed to be. And, by the same token, a reappraisal of what a rule or a law was deemed to be. There can be no self without rules, and vice versa. Wilde writes as though people might forget that they had a so-called self, that he or she had his or her own thoughts, personality and development; and that this was what the laws they lived by had led them to (as though conformity had become the new individualism). Wilde's aestheticism, in other words, was an attempt to avert the elegiac; to persuade people to always prefer the next good thing. He wanted what his near-contemporary Nietzsche called 'more life'; his object of desire, again like Nietzsche, was the future, not the past.

With less earnestness, and far less portentousness, Wilde was – in Zarathustra's words from Nietzsche's great book – not sitting and waiting like the prophetic Zarathustra, but talking and writing, 'with old shattered tablets around [him] as well as new half-inscribed tablets'. But Wilde, like Nietzsche (like everyone else) could speak the language of the future only by using in new ways the language of the past. Neither of them wanted any more tablets of law, any more exact and overexacting commandments of good and evil. And both of them realized that all tablets are only ever half inscribed, always to be completed, and never to be completable, in what are always unknowable futures. That morality – and morality is only ever the language in which it finds its form – could no longer be used to stop time. Or talk. Or development. If God is dead, the phrase 'become who you are', as used by Nietzsche and endorsed in a different way by Wilde (as 'the full realization of his own personality'), necessarily involves, in another of Nietzsche's phrases, 'a transvaluation of all values'. 'Who you are' no longer means who you have been essentially defined as by an omniscient authority. The forbidden begins to lose its grip; or one set of forbidden things simply replaces another. For both Nietzsche and Wilde, man, as he was then called, is the evaluating animal, not merely the obedient animal. So the questions were no longer which of man's evaluations are true, but rather, what is he doing when he is evaluating? Or, not what is forbidden, and why, but rather, why is this forbidden now, and to what purpose? Who is doing the forbidding, and who is consenting, and what kind of pleasure does it give them? What is the making forbidden a way of doing? What are we making when we make something forbidden, when we lay down the law in no uncertain terms?

To forbid can be both protective and intimidating, superstitious and realistic, sadistic and masochistic, vengeful and comforting, imaginative and narrow-minded, optimistic and pessimistic, terrified, arrogant, kind, omniscient and humble. Without the forbidden as traditionally conceived, in other words – the forbidden as that which, because it must not be contested, apparently can't be contested – we lose all our preferred dramas. We lose a hallowed vocabulary (unforbidden pleasures pale in comparison). When Wilde and Nietzsche in their different ways ask us to talk differently about the forbidden and the forbidders, they ask us to consider our pleasures anew. If religion and its structures of moral authority were to be no longer objects of desire – and towards the end of the nineteenth century, unlike today, this seemed like a distinct possibility – where could those desires be satisfied, or how could the desires themselves change, or be modified? Could we want new things, and in different ways? What would wanting be like if other things were forbidden – if, say, 'vulgarity', or 'dullness', or 'earnestness' were forbidden, as both Wilde and Nietzsche would have preferred – or even if there were no things we were forbidden to want? We do not have laws because we have desires: we have desires because we have laws, they want us to believe. The law arranges our wanting for us. These were the kinds of intimations of mortality that the new writing of the later nineteenth century was beginning to encourage. Wilde and Nietzsche, and later Freud (among others), allowed us to wonder, in an interestingly secular way, what it was that the forbidders wanted, and why we had needed to deify them in order to take them seriously.

V

'Man feels himself to be a more various and richly-endowed animal than the old religious theory of human life allowed,' Matthew Arnold wrote in a letter to Ernest Fontanès in March 1881, 'and he is endeavouring to give satisfaction to the long suppressed and still imperfectly-understood instincts of this varied nature.' Arnold is clear that something is dawning which has been, in his view, 'long suppressed', (and suppressed primarily by Christianity), and which modern Darwinian biology is allowing people to recognize in new ways. What has been suppressed, in Arnold's view, is something of the sensual spontaneity, the life-affirming intellectual curiosity of the ancient Greeks (the Greeks, that is, as Arnold and some of his contemporaries conceived them to be). Instincts and their satisfaction are now the issue, not faith and doubt, or duty and compassion, or morality and grace. And the instincts are not so much new as long buried. A 'more various and richly-endowed animal' is at once expansive, unfrightened and full of excited apprehension; there is no mention of selves or souls. Arnold is announcing a renaissance of something both ancient and unprecedented.

There is, in one of the old religious theories of human life, a self made by God, which is living for this God who lays down the laws of life. But once people begin to feel and believe that they may be what Arnold calls, 'more various and richly-endowed' animals – animals, that is to say, as described by Darwin, among others, and therefore no longer selves in the traditional sense – they have to imagine what a self not made by God, not providentially informed, might be like; and how, if at all, the word 'self' still applies. And, by the same token, they have to ask what a law is like, and its laying down, when it is imposed not by a god but by a human animal. And with this, of course, comes the possibility that our so-called selves might be quite different from the divinely created selves that we have inherited (that is, that we have been persuaded to believe in); and, indeed, that being or having a self may be just one among many ways of describing what we are.

We are all too familiar by now with a wide-ranging scepticism about what, if anything, the word 'self' (or 'individual') can refer to, or include and preclude; and about what hidden agendas the idea of the self can be used to sponsor or maintain (what old, religious theory of human life the self, and all the assumptions about the self, might bring in its wake). And we are also becoming familiar with descriptive vocabularies – in some versions of psychoanalysis, in structuralism, in neurobiology – that can, and want to, dispense with the term 'self' altogether (though not to dispense, it seems, with the laying down of laws). As though, for example, the anachronism of the self may be keeping us in some sense religious, connected to those selves that were created, and as part of a sacred order; at once too servile and too arrogant, too knowing and too serious, too reverential and too defiant, too self-important and too self-deceiving. As though the Judeo-Christian God and the selves He supposedly made were really a radically misleading picture of – the wrong, or out-dated, vocabulary for – the kind of creatures we are, the kind of creatures we were turning out to be, or wanted to be; creatures that evolved, creatures that could be more or less self-fashioning (Nietzsche's injunction, 'become who you are' depends entirely on the language you have for what you might be, or take yourself to be). This, at least, is what the names Wilde, Nietzsche and Freud, among many others, stand for in the great nineteenth-century awakening, in which directions for a possible and unprecedented secularism are beginning to be worked out. And what is at stake is how, if at all, the competing accounts of what a person is, and what a life, and indeed a good life, entails, can be linked up. And whether a compelling account can be given of who people are in terms of what they want, or feel the lack of, an account which capitalism exploited in a particular way.

In psychoanalysis – a discipline contemporary, in its beginnings, with other traditions of aestheticism, and significantly and strangely influenced by Nietzsche; a discipline trying to put together pleasure and morality in new ways – the use of the word 'self' can feel like a throwback, a nostalgic, almost regressive, attempt to unify the ineluctably conflicted individual that Freud described (as, indeed, in their different ways, had Wilde and Nietzsche). Freud frightened even psychoanalysts with his unconventional (that is, secular) description of a person as having everything except a self – instincts, conscience, an ego, but nothing that could put it all together, nothing that could use the word 'I' with conviction or any kind of real authority. Psychoanalysis could help us forget the self, and help us talk about conflicting desires and punitive internal authorities instead; or competing pleasures; or competing evaluations of pleasure, a Death Instinct that wants to destroy the possibility of pleasure, and a Life Instinct that will go to great lengths to sustain pleasure (once again there being no single sovereign authority). It could encourage us, at its most unsettling, to allow for a great deal of disarray and drive, of incoherence and unintelligibility, of pleasure found at all costs. Like Wilde and Nietzsche, Freud was to urge on us a newish vocabulary that would make us wonder what we are doing in moralizing ourselves and others; what kind of pleasure moralizing was; how the forbidden forbids us the language to talk and think about what we are doing when we forbid; and why we might be wanting one God rather than many; and why we would be wanting any gods at all.

Freud would redescribe 'good' and 'evil' – or Wilde's language of the 'beautiful' and the 'vulgar', or 'ugly' – as, initially, the more blandly secular (and bodily) 'acceptable' and 'unacceptable', what we can take in and what we can't swallow and want to spit out. And then, later in our development, he would describe us as internalizing our parents' versions of good and evil, the 'superego' being Freud's new word for the part of ourselves that forbids us what we most want and mustn't have (the superego guarding us against and punishing us for the incestuous desires of the Oedipus complex). He would see us as riddled with severe, unduly punitive and forbidding internal authorities that we use to obscure ourselves, to hide and even attack the versions of ourselves that may matter most to us. For Freud, any moral clarity we have is a temporary suppression of the complexity of our desires. Morality, as Wilde and Nietzsche would also say, was a servile over-simplification of ourselves in the service of self-protection. Freud's psychoanalysis would be an attempt to work out an alternative to this protection racket. And for Freud, as for Wilde and Nietzsche, amusement was somehow the key. Certain kinds of pleasure, usually previously forbidden, had to be recycled. And certain things needed to be forgotten so that certain other things could be remembered instead.

So we should note that of Freud's two references to Wilde in his work one of them links Nietzsche and Wilde together. In, appropriately enough, *The Psychopathology of Everyday Life* (1901), Freud referred to a patient that his colleague Sándor Ferenczi had told him about: 'A lady,' he wrote, 'who had heard something about psychoanalysis, could not recall the name of the psychiatrist Jung. The following names came to her mind instead', among them Wilde and Nietzsche. Freud continued:

> As a common characterization of Wilde and Nietzsche she named 'insanity'. Then she said chaffingly: 'You Freudians will go on looking for the causes of insanity until you are insane yourselves.' Then: 'I can't bear Wilde and Nietzsche. I don't understand them. I hear they were both homosexuals. Wilde had dealings with young people.'

Freud reports this – and it is, of course, of interest that he wants Nietzsche and Wilde named in his text, and linked in this way – in a section of his book about what he calls 'the forgetting of names' and the 'motives' for such forgettings. I want to suggest that Wilde, Nietzsche and Freud himself were all, in their different ways, encouraging the forgetting of certain names and the wish to replace these forgotten names with other names ('goodness' replaced by 'beauty', 'duty' replaced by 'delight', 'punishment' by 'sexual pleasure', and so on). And, unsurprisingly, as Freud unconsciously suggests, this was considered, even by them, as somehow disreputable and disturbing (insane, homosexual, paedophiliac). As the patient says, looking for the causes of insanity could make you insane. This was what Wilde called the 'strange influence' of words. You forget one word and you come up with another. One word leads to another. You forget a name (Jung) and the next thing you know you are talking about paedophilia. The patient got from Jung to the young via Wilde and Nietzsche. The forgetting of names and what they might be replaced by – what the forgetting might lead you into – was clearly dangerous. When you lose one intention you always find some more. Forgetting, Freud would suggest, was a way forward. Only by forgetting a name can you come up with another one.

VI

When Nietzsche wanted to describe the day the world changed in *Thus Spoke Zarathustra*, he invented the day of an ultimate forgetting, the day when God forgot Himself. In the history of the forgetting of names this was one day, Nietzsche believed, that should stand out. Indeed, on the day that God, the one Judeo-Christian God, forgot Himself, all the other gods died – of laughter. This, at least, is Nietzsche's fable of the end of the old religions, and perhaps, Nietzsche hopes, the death of religions altogether and their vocabulary of what he calls 'life-hatred', 'world-hatred', 'world-slander'. In this book that is, in the words of philosopher Robert Pippin in his *Introductions to Nietzsche*, 'both a prophetic book and a kind of send-up of a prophetic book' that both presents Zarathustra as 'a teacher and [parodies] his attempt to play that role' – that is to say, not unlike many of Wilde's fictions – we have to be as attentive to tone as to content. The sounds of words and voices make their own kind of sense; and tone can be at odds with intended meanings (another meaning of Wilde's 'strange influence' of language, and one that Freud endorses). 'For with the old Gods things came to an end long ago,' Nietzsche wrote in the section entitled 'On Apostates':

>   – and verily, they had a good and
>   joyful Gods' end!
>
> Theirs was no mere 'twilight' death – that is a lie!
> Rather: one day they – *laughed* themselves to death!
>
> This happened when the most godless words issued
> from a God himself – the words: 'There is one God!
> Thou shalt have no other God before me!' –
>
> – an old wrath-beard of a God, most jealous, forgot
> himself thus: –
>
> And thereupon all the Gods laughed and rocked on
> their chairs and shouted: 'Is just this not Godliness,
> that there are Gods, but no God?'
>
> He that hath ears let him hear.

In Exodus 20:3–5, God introduces the Ten Commandments by saying, 'Thou shalt have no other gods before me . . . For I the Lord thy God am a jealous God.' This is what makes them the commandments that they are supposed to be; not guidelines, or suggestions, or talking points, but a list of unarguably forbidden things. This is the canonical formulation of the idea of living for others prescribed by what we might call our most significant other. In the Ten Commandments it is made explicit both what and who we are living for. It is the idea of there being one law that is clearly anathema, so to speak, to Nietzsche and his pagan gods. But the idea of the only God as a jealous god is itself something of a giveaway; as though the joke was on God without His realizing it. If God was really omniscient and omnipotent He would have nothing to be jealous about, so the qualification seems unnecessary. Jealousy, one could say, is the real acknowledgement that there are other gods; and that if there are other gods one may not be the God that one thought one was.

The 'Gods' end' was not a 'mere "twilight" death', as in Wagner's Ring Cycle – Wagner having been one of the young Nietzsche's gods, but now dead to him as an idol – it was nothing so serious, so portentous. Indeed, it was a laughing matter. God forgot Himself by laying down the law – the law of His own unique sovereignty that invalidates all other authority. By misnaming Himself He had misnamed everyone else as well. It was, at least in Wilde's terms, the ultimate selfishness of needing everyone to agree with you.

For the pagan gods, godliness was by definition polytheism; a conflict and collaboration between essentially hedonistic deities (like Wilde, and in a sense Freud, Nietzsche took his moral and aesthetic compass from the ancient Greeks – though each of them, of course, had a different ancient Greece). So when the Judeo-Christian God declares His unique sovereignty, the other gods, the earlier gods, can only burst out laughing at the absurdity

of His claim, its self-importance, its arrogance, its tyrannical cruelty, its patent and ridiculous untruth. As Blake
was to write in *The Marriage of Heaven and Hell*, in words
that Nietzsche and Wilde would clearly have endorsed,
'one law for the lion and ox is oppression'. Nietzsche's fable
includes, of course, a nice homey picture of the gods rock-
ing on their chairs, as if to say: those pagan gods were
much more like us; whereas this God of the old and new
tablets is a monster! He'd never burst out laughing and
rock on His chair! Why, though, would this pronouncement finish off all the gods, albeit with amusement? And
why does Nietzsche suggest that God 'forgot' Himself in
making this pronouncement? What would He have said if
He had remembered Himself?

Nietzsche is saying, I think, that this declaration by
God of His unique omnipotence and omniscience makes
a mockery of the whole notion of deity. It exposes the
ambitions of deity and therefore exposes the worst ambitions of men. It is as if Nietzsche is saying: when I propose
the 'overcoming of the human' – Nietzsche's abiding
preoccupation – I am not proposing that we should become
in any way like our gods; in fact our gods, whom we have
invented, should be our negative ideals when it comes to
our ambitions for ourselves; when we forget ourselves –
forget our best or preferred selves – we are likely to say

things like 'There is one God! Thou shalt have no other gods before ME!' When we are autocratic, tyrannical and arrogant – when, that is to say, we are being a certain version of forbidding – we are actively attacking our better self; when we lay down the law as the only law, we have become lawless (the outlaw as psychopath). We have been corrupted (or misled, waylaid) in Nietzsche's view, by the wrong vocabulary, the wrong picture of what it is to be fully alive (in Wilde's terms we need to recover our best selfishness by redescribing the bad press selfishness has traditionally been given). The 'exemplars', to use Nietzsche's word, that we seek are those people, not gods, who enable us to become who we are. God, in Nietzsche's fabulation, forgot Himself, and even His own name; He thought He was God, THE God, when He was simply one among many others (inner superiority means we are on the wrong track, it means we are too intimidated). 'With you,' his Shadow says to Zarathustra,

> 'I strove to enter everything forbidden, the worst, and farthest: and if there is anything of virtue in me, it is that I have feared no prohibition.
>
> 'With you I shattered whatever my heart had revered . . .
>
> 'With you I unlearned my belief in words and values and great names.'

It was the unlearning of the greatest name of all, God, that Zarathustra taught; and the torrent of unnaming that this unleashed. And this great unnaming, this shattering of whatever the heart had revered, would make people prone, as Nietzsche knew, to recovering themselves with new narrowings of the mind. 'Beware that some narrow belief, a harsh, severe illusion, does not catch you in the end!' Zarathustra warns his Shadow. 'For you are now seduced and tempted by anything that is narrow and firm.' If we give up one set of laws, Nietzsche warns us, we are likely to be tempted to pick up another similar set of laws, but to call them new. Our freedom may be merely a new version of our old confinement. And what we can't give up or get over is our desire for the law, for something 'narrow and firm', to keep us in place; as though the laws never really change because our desire for particular kinds of laws remains the same. We can never quite get over our fear of ourselves. But we have been made unduly fearful of ourselves, Nietzsche suggests, by those very laws we have consented to. Or rather, more realistically, we don't know how fearful we should be of ourselves, as we haven't given ourselves the opportunity to find out. The law forbids being open to an open future; the open future of who we may be, and of who we may want to be.

VII

We have inherited the wrong picture, the wrong vocabulary, for authority, power, vitality, pleasure and language. Laying down this kind of law for ourselves and others is a betrayal of what Nietzsche wants human beings to be (Wilde's God would say, why not develop your colour-sense? Nietzsche's God would say, why are we all so obsessed by valuation, by all these old names? Freud's God would say, only people who don't want to grow up need gods). There are names we should start wanting to forget, or to unlearn (two different things that need not always be so different); Nietzsche urges us in the Preface to *The Gay Science*, the book that preceded *Thus Spoke Zarathustra*, 'to learn as artists to forget well, to be good at not knowing!' (which lets us wonder what the difference is between forgetting and unlearning). By forgetting a name we can come up with another one (Freud says, don't think about gods, think about parents: and then, when you forget about parents, see what you come up with). The patient wanted to think of Jung but was lucky or unlucky enough to think of Wilde and Nietzsche instead. What do we need to forget to say something new? Well, we may need to do that forbidden thing, to forget about the forbidden, at least sometimes and in various different ways. To forget at least some versions of the forbidden and to come up with other names instead. 'Those with originality,' Nietzsche wrote in *The Gay Science*, 'have usually been the name-givers'. That is, the name-changers.

The American philosopher James Conant, in his remarkable essay 'Nietzsche's Perfectionism', having acknowledged, along with other contemporary philosophers, that Nietzsche's philosophy is itself a kind of aestheticism – an attempt to find another language for traditional moralities, to find new names and new pleasures for an old ethics – suggests that Nietzsche's 'abiding preoccupation (and his evident desire to instil in the reader a similar preoccupation)' is,

with questions concerning what one should value – questions such as, 'What sort of person [or persons] should I admire (and what sort of response should such admiration elicit in me)?' 'How should I live (if I wish to be worthy of such admiration myself)?' And, 'In what ways (and by what means) should I endeavour to shape and change myself?'

We don't, in the ordinary way of things, talk about remembering ourselves; we talk about forgetting ourselves, either in states of absorption or when we think of ourselves as having acted out of character. As though the self itself – the 'self' as an idea, as a word – could be forgotten but not remembered. And then, when 'it' is forgotten, new things begin to happen. Conant's pertinent questions that he takes Nietzsche to be asking suggest something akin to a need to keep ourselves, or something about ourselves, in mind; and particularly to keep in mind the relationship between our self at the moment and our as yet unattained self, our always potentially better self that we are wanting to become. He doesn't, we can't help but notice, dispense with the idea of the self, but he does account for the self as wanting always to be something else, something better, something other than it is. It is as though 'it' exists only in its transitions; it exists only in a changing, in an aspiring, state. And in describing the self as being preoccupied in this way – in wanting, in Nietzsche's language, to be 'overcoming' itself: to go further with itself but not to try to become something it isn't – he leaves us wondering what law is being laid down here, what are the rules, so to speak, for becoming the as yet unattained self? 'We teach people how to remember, we never teach them how to grow,' Wilde wrote in 'The Critic as Artist'. The law is that which we must remember. What – or which names – do we need to be able to forget about in order to overcome ourselves, in order to grow? Or, to put it another way: what are we being when we are being obedient? And what are we doing to ourselves?

Tricks of Obedience

We cannot ask others to accept our history as their own.
Paul W. Kahn, *Putting Liberalism in Its Place*

I

If disobedience can be a forbidden pleasure, obedience can be an unforbidden one. Without forbidden pleasure, by definition, there can be no disobedience; without obedience it is not quite so clear what there can be. And so we need to wonder what kind of pleasure obedience might be, craved and courted as it often is, fought for and fought with. No one can be indifferent, no one can be nonchalant, about their own obedience, a gift for obedience and its refusal being where we start from, and what we start with. 'Before nourishment there must be obedience,' the poet Eduardo C. Corral writes in his poem 'Slow Lightning',

48

suggesting that something we might be unwilling to describe as 'obedience' may even be the precondition for our survival, for our being able to take in what we need. So when it comes to obedience, in anyone's life, there will be no slow lightening of the burdens and complications it entails. One's personal history, whatever else it is, is a history of one's obedience. For everyone, the retrospective question is always, what did I consent to, and what did I have to submit to, as a child, that I didn't actually agree with? Whether one wants to do what one is told to do – that is, whether one wants what one is told to want – and what we can do with and about this question, are the moral starting points. All moral questions are questions of obedience.

Whether it refers to 'the action or practice of obeying' in the reassuringly neutral initial definition of the *Oxford English Dictionary*, or to the at once more alarming and reassuring further definition of obedient as 'submissive to the will of a superior; doing what one is bidden; subservient; dutiful', it is clear what the word itself springs us into. Whom we obey and how we obey – and what we are doing when we obey – will be the defining factors in our lives, from the very beginning to the more or less bitter end. It is a question of who we take to be superior and why, and what this involves us in; and how we use the old-fashioned vocabulary of 'inferior' and 'superior', and why these might be the terms we are tempted to use. What kinds of obedience are required of us to get what we need is as pressing a question in infancy as it will be in old age. What our obedience turns us into – the difference between self-betrayal and whatever we take to be its opposite – will be every bit as significant as what it takes out of us.

The word 'obedience' itself makes us think about legitimacy, about the pleasures of being agreeable, about what following a rule can lead you into: an unthinking compliance, say, or a desired state of intimidation; a delight in conformity; the pleasures of being part of a group; or a moral masochism; authenticity or self-travesty. When Edmund Burke wrote in 1757 that someone's 'idea even of liberty was not (if I may use the expression) perfectly free' ('An Essay Towards an Abridgement of the English History'), he was alerting the English-reading public to the inevitable compromises even in the idea of freedom. Who, Burke wants us to wonder, has 'perfect liberty', and what would that be like? What would it be to, as it were, take a perfect liberty?

An interesting history of morality, of self-fashioning and its discontents, could be traced through the fluctuating uses and connotations of the word 'obedience', and the thoughts of obligation and liberation it always brings in its wake (so it is of significance, for example, when the disobedient adolescent is secretly admired, though publicly discredited; or when obedience is a pejorative but being rule-abiding might not be). Obedience has its virtues and its vices; and a lot of cultural work goes into putting obedience in its place. Indeed, the ways in which the word is used are always a sign of the times. The obedient, as Samuel Johnson defines them in his 1755 dictionary – which is more or less contemporary with my quotation from Burke – are 'submissive to authority; compliant with command or prohibition; obsequious'. If we are not submissive to authority, what can we be to it? Preferably not obsequious. And what can we be to it without it ceasing to be authority at all? Especially if, to take the obvious case, the authority is God? For Johnson, an eighteenth-century British Anglican Tory, 'compliant' can mean, in his dictionary, 'civil'; and a 'complier' is 'a man of an easy temper'. For the twentieth-century British paediatrician and psychoanalyst D. W. Winnicott, a man of Dissenter stock, what is to be feared in early development is 'that the infant shall give up spontaneity in favour of compliance with the needs of those who are caring for the infant'; and as he wrote in *The Family and Individual Development*, he is justly reassured when a five-month-old infant 'did not pass over into a compliant state, which would have meant that she had given up hope'. The idea of passing over into a compliant state equates compliance with a kind of death; a death-in-life in which the child survives at the cost of living her own life. For Johnson, compliance can be a mark of appropriate sociability, of successful adaptation; for Winnicott, it is the opposite. For Johnson, the political and theological implications of the word are explicit; in Winnicott, they are implicit. For Johnson, accommodation is the order of the day; for Winnicott, the accommodating are unaccommodated, bereft of their own desire, all dressed up with nowhere to go (madness, Winnicott wrote, is the need to be believed). For Winnicott, compliance is a sign of what he calls the 'False Self'; for Johnson, it can be a sign of what he doesn't call the true self. To be obedient can mean being overcompliant (what Johnson calls 'obsequious'). Or it can mean obeying the right master, the right rules, the right laws, the right God. The old names redescribed become new names; the same words are used to do quite different things. In these eighteenth-century usages, to 'submit' can be to acknowledge a true hierarchy, and in the twentieth century it can mean to be unduly intimidated. The same words, changing over time, encourage us to lead different kinds of lives. The histories of these particular words, 'liberty', 'submission', 'compliance', 'obedience', ask us who and what we should believe, and how we should do our believing. They ask us what our reasons might be for forbidding ourselves certain things, for consenting without ever quite knowing what we are consenting to.

The first person we believe – whether we believe her or not – is, in Winnicott's view, the mother (or the unfortunately named 'caretaker'). In the worst-case scenario, in the words of Frank Bidart's poem 'By These Waters', 'What begins in recognition, – . . . ends in obedience.' The infant literally depends on the mother's recognition of his need, and if the mother is, for her own good reasons, excessively unreceptive to the nature of his need, he will have to adapt to her limits, to her capacity for recognition; to try to become what she needs him to be. But, like all of us – and to varying degrees, and the degrees matter and are fateful – the infant will have to want what the mother wants him to want. What is recognized in him, what he is seen to be, he will have to become obedient to (unlike Wilde's 'Artist'). When the mother says to the child, 'Do you want apple juice or orange juice?', the compliant, obedient child will always choose one of the two; the non-compliant child faced with this choice will have the mental space to wonder what else, if anything, he would rather have to drink. The obedient child is too fearful of the mother to have more of a mind of his own than she can acknowledge. It is then effectively forbidden to think outside of the mother's terms. The child becomes someone who when he is thirsty – or worse, when he is distressed – likes either apple juice or orange juice; he becomes that kind of person. Those are the names he remembers. What begins in recognition ends in obedience. The child tacitly consents to a life of being fobbed off. The child who is at first caught and held in the mother's vocabulary can end up being trapped in it (leaving home means learning to talk differently from your parents). And in this sense obedience always takes the form of obedience to a specific vocabulary. It can be comforting to be trapped in other people's descriptions of oneself – and the infant is more or less his parents' descriptions of him – but it is also exceedingly frustrating. Or rather, it is exceedingly frustrating if you are brought up in a culture that also encourages self-definition and distrusts excessive adaptation; that promotes certain individualistic versions of the flourishing self; or that even talks about something called a 'self', that a person both is and can become even more of. In these cultures the individual is always left wondering, what are the pleasures I have been deprived of? How have I failed to develop? Have I lived by the wrong rules, the wrong picture of what a life ought to be? Who is having more or better pleasure than I am? How have they got it and how

do they do it? What would my life have been like if I had
been a different person with different parents? Or, to put
it in Frank Bidart's more curious terms, do all forms of
recognition end up as forms of obedience? As if to be seen
is always and only to have a picture of oneself to live up
to. This is what psychoanalysis, following on from the
more secular, liberal forms of nineteenth-century education and the more or less secular forms of aestheticism,
was invented to talk about: what language makes possible
for an animal (a self, a history, a project, chaos). Without
language we wouldn't even know that we existed, or that
we had possibilities.

II

The overcompliant, obedient child that Winnicott describes
has the pleasure of short-term safety; he is keeping the
mother going by making demands that are well within
what he takes to be the mother's range (he is not being a
difficult child; he is keeping the mother happy, not strain-
ing her). The non-compliant child is free to find out what
the mother's range might be, and, by the same token, what
his range might be. The compliant child resigns himself;
the non-compliant child risks himself: the compliant child

consolidates; the non-compliant child experiments. Rebels keep the world the same so they can go on rebelling against it, Sartre says; revolutionaries change the world. The compliant child runs the risk of becoming a rebel; the non-compliant child runs the risk of wanting a permanent state of revolution, of more or less continual self-overcoming. The compliant child, in this very modern story, will crave ritual and routine; the non-compliant child will want nothing but the shock of the new (anger is hope: hope that things can be different; that frustration can be modified). The non-compliant child is always wanting to extend her repertoire; the compliant child is wanting more of the same.

And yet, of course, as we try to place ourselves on this list, it is abundantly clear that, where we would like there to be opposites and contraries, there are always blurrings and blendings. At its most banal we can say, we are probably always a bit of both; that these distinctions are satisfying in their simplifying clarity. That we all both complied with our mothers and protested (and are probably still doing so); and with our fathers also. We all wanted to help, cure and console our parents and we all wanted to ruin their lives if we needed to, and so on. But it is also true, I think, that the whole notion of obedience itself oversimplifies, and that that is its function: that when we talk about obedience – and all our cultural conversations have been, in one sense, about nothing else – we are drawn to make confoundingly sharp distinctions. And all in the name of clarity. God and Satan, Church and State, desire and duty, law and justice, private and public: obedience has meant having and wanting to choose, and not wanting to have to choose; having to declare allegiances without being free enough to think about them; the whole notion of obedience tending to reinforce the pleasures of mutual exclusion (to forbid something is to define it). Or rather, perhaps, obedience has been staged in a way that invites us to make impossible choices (in the view of Nietzsche and Wilde we have sacrificed our unknowable multiplicitly by serving such limited gods); choices that divide us against ourselves in unnecessarily self-mutilating ways, and are in that sense false choices (a false choice is one in which we must give up something we deem to be essential, and have to be impressed that we are able to do so). Obedience, that is to say, is the mother of tragedy; if obedience is what we need – at least in its absolutist forms, and you can't really be a bit obedient, any more than you can be a bit pregnant – then tragedy is what we are going to get. Tragic heroes have an absolute, unarguable obedience to their own beliefs. All tragedies are tragedies of obedience.

Obedience is the unforbidden pleasure that gives us something by forbidding us something else – something often of ultimate value. At its most minimal it forbids us from thinking about the pleasures our obedience might exclude. It narrows our minds, narrows our picture of ourselves as believing and believable people. And so we can see the ways in which obedience is that paradoxical thing: an apparently unforbidden pleasure that is essentially forbidding. The most pernicious unforbidden pleasures are the ones that are forbidden (and forbidding) pleasures in disguise. As a god might say (or a certain kind of parent): 'If you are obedient to me I will love and protect and guarantee your life; but this depends upon, this entails, your consenting to everything I forbid.' Obedience becomes the unforbidden pleasure that forbids so much. And that, indeed, creates a forbidden world.

III

To successfully forbid something requires a certain amount of intimidation; indeed, the forbidden depends upon it (it is worth wondering why morality without intimidation is inconceivable; or what the story is that we tell ourselves about morality that makes intimidation integral). But the forbidden can also depend upon the intimidation being disguised as something else – protectiveness, chosenness, destiny, love; obedience here signifying being loved, chosen, protected, destined in some way. Obedience, then, is an unforbidden pleasure sponsored by the forbidden pleasure of intimidation. Unforbidden pleasures, therefore, have nothing to do with intimidation (nothing to do with it in both senses: they are neither intimidating, nor do they require intimidation to sustain them). Whereas intimidation has everything to do with forbidden pleasures. So the questions become: when and why, in any given situation, is intimidation required? And, what are the very real pleasures of being intimidated? And the complement to each of these questions respectively is: what does it say about any belief if it requires menace to enforce it? And what is it about the pleasure of being intimidated that makes it so often our preferred pleasure? Intimidation becomes necessary when collaboration is despaired of. We have all, of course, tried to master the fears of childhood, and we may want to go on proving to ourselves that we can survive our terrors; this is itself both addictive and the root of that addiction (addiction is always the ongoing attempt to survive what was experienced as malign mothering, the mothering to which one had to submit). Making the case for unforbidden pleasures must involve being able to answer these questions – questions about pleasure and intimidation; it must involve giving good reasons for being so impressed by the forbidden. Because it is conceivable that we might learn to enjoy pleasures other than the pleasures of being terrorized.

'In the actual historical world of existing societies,' Rowan Williams writes in *Faith in the Public Square*, 'the good is something that gets argued about . . . If the state does indeed have a kind of moral interest . . . it is twofold – an interest in securing the liberty of groups to pursue their own social goods, and an interest in building in to its own processes a set of cautions and defences against absolutism.' For the good to be something that gets argued about, as Williams knows, both the state and the individual's inner state have to be conducive. And, of course, if the good is something that gets argued about it should not lead to obedience: obedience would mean the end of the argument, or that the argument had been prematurely concluded. Obedience here would be a refuge or a retreat from the argument. The argument, in one way or another, would have been forbidden ('A conversation that would otherwise continue without end,' Paul W. Kahn writes in *Political Theology*, 'is brought to an end only by imagining an omniscient figure'). Obedience is always a conversation stopper. Or, to put it psychoanalytically, it is the saboteur of free association (free speech at its most incoherent, unpredictable and revealing).

So to begin with we can put it like this: obedience; or argument and free association. Both, of course, requiring obedience. Both there to help us get the lives we want, or the lives someone else wants us to want. Both means to quite different ends, to put it more instrumentally. Obedience, like free association, comes with a promise. To be obedient, though, you need something or someone to obey; to free associate you need only obey the demand that you free associate. If you are obedient to X, Y will supposedly happen (if you love and obey God you will, or could, be saved); if you free associate in the presence of an analyst, your suffering will, or could, be modified (it's actually anyone's guess what will happen once you start to free associate, though some people – the psychoanalytic officials – will say they do more or less know). Belief, then, is a form of prophecy: it offers to tell you something about your future self. Free association, or obedience in its various forms – they may both come with their promises, but as with all promises we can't help but wonder what, if anything, they can guarantee.

'To learn what a man's moral beliefs are,' Stuart Hampshire writes in his essay 'Morality and Pessimism', 'entails learning what he thinks that he must not do, at any cost or at almost any cost.' A person's moral beliefs are exposed in what he believes he must not do. To be obedient you must not disobey; and you must not argue beyond a certain point about what or who you must obey. To free associate, in psychoanalysis, you must not stop yourself speaking, and you must be willing to talk about why you may have stopped talking when you do. In psychoanalysis, that is to say, you learn something about your resistance to obedience, and your resistance to disobedience. But psychoanalysis, whatever else it is, involves talking about what we must not do, with a view to reconsidering whether or not we should do it. And it therefore acknowledges that what we must not do at almost any cost always comes at a cost. Psychoanalysis is a conversation, sometimes an argument, in which that cost can be considered. Psychoanalytic treatment is one of the cultural forms people can use to talk about their obedience.

The forbidden is traditionally the enemy of conversation about the forbidden; it is the unarguable (so when politics becomes a forbidden pleasure it is anti-democratic). What is forbidden cannot, by definition, be argued about. It must not be described from different points of view, redescribed, or mocked. It must be taken on its own terms and it must never be forgotten. The way to understand the forbidden, Hampshire intimates, is to understand something about what it is costing us.

IV

Obedience and freer association – and the question of to whom or to what one might be being obedient in the desire for freer association – are the themes of both the Genesis myth and John Milton's more equivocal rewriting of the Genesis myth in *Paradise Lost* (1667) (if Genesis had been the last word, Milton would not have felt the need to revisit it). But in both the story is one in which unforbidden pleasures are sacrificed for forbidden pleasures; although forbidden pleasures have always coexisted with unforbidden pleasures in the Garden of Eden, so we think of them as belonging together, and always wonder about their relationship with each other. In the Genesis story, unforbidden pleasures come first and are found to be insufficient. But insufficient for what? What are the unforbidden pleasures depriving Adam and Eve of? All they know before the Fall is that there is something they must not do, which means there is something they must not want. But knowing this makes it known (and wanted); they needn't, after all, have been told, and then presumably they would not have known not simply *what* they were missing, but that there *was* something they were missing. So in the beginning was a tantalization. A temptation was created. And it was created by a demand for obedience; obedience being required because its alternative is worse – whatever that alternative is assumed to be; it being the function of obedience to persuade us that there is no real, no viable, alternative.

It could be construed that Adam and Eve had, for example, been fobbed off with the all too available, all too accessible, unforbidden pleasures before the so-called Fall; as though the unforbidden was something you could fall out of, and the forbidden was what you then fell into; or as though the unforbidden couldn't hold them, couldn't hold their attention. And as though the forbidden was a terminal distraction. Once it was named it couldn't be renamed or unnamed (it was something, we now might say, that couldn't be repressed: it was in a different category from all those things that can be repressed). And it couldn't be merely endlessly thought about or imagined; it had to be, as we say, acted upon. So something was sacrificed, or at least given up, and something else was gained. Indeed, what actually happened is an ironic commentary on Hampshire's appropriately entitled essay 'Morality and Pessimism': in learning about morality, Adam and Eve learned about pessimism. By doing what they must not do at any cost, they discovered morality. They may have had a morality beforehand – or at least a way of life – but it was organized around what they must not do at any cost or, as they might have imagined, at almost any cost. After they had done what they must not at any cost do, they switched it for a new kind of morality – and pessimism was at the heart of it. It cost Adam and Eve their previous life. But now, at least, they had done the worst, and they could discover, for better and for worse, what their life was like in the aftermath of the Fall, instead of what it was like in anticipation of eating that fruit. Real morality for them could begin only after the worst thing had happened, or rather, after they had done the worst thing. And so it might be for us. If it turned out that you were capable of even worse things, you would then have reason to doubt your God. Unless, of course, all of the worse things are deemed to be the consequence of the Fall, which they were. People, even then, were capable of far worse things than anything Adam and Eve did in the Garden of Eden; but in this story there could be no worse thing than this particular disobedience, which made people monstrous. So disobedience – this particular disobedience – was once and for ever the worst thing people can do. This could make people prize obedience above everything else.

After the Fall there could only be, at best, mixed blessings. After the Fall, for example, you can have an unconscious; before the Fall we didn't need one. After the Fall we could have conversations, arguments, about the good, about morality (which now exists). After the Fall we knew just how bad we could be. We knew what evil was. 'A human being,' Hampshire writes, 'has the power to reflect on what kind of person he wants to be, and to try to act accordingly, within the limits of his circumstances.' But this is true only after the Fall. Before the Fall there was no such thing as the person we might want to be.

In the beginning there was a tantalization, and then a disobedience. Adam and Eve, we could say, had to put a stop to the tantalization. And everything followed on from there (including the fact that the tantalization can never be stopped, only modified). And, the psychoanalyst can add, everything since depends upon what the child can do with, and about, the ineluctably tantalizing mother. In the beginning there is always the mother, who is experienced by the child as tantalizing, whether she wants to be or not. She promises so much, even all there is, but is only ever more or less predictably available. And so then there is always the obedience and the disobedience, the deal and the protest ('I'll be good if you'll be there' as opposed to 'I want you as and when I want you'). So before we turn to another paradise lost we can say, from a psychoanalytic point of view, that there is the malign obedience of the defeated child: what Johnson called 'obsequiousness', and what we might also call arrogance – with all the rage they both entail. And then there is the more benign, the more promising, obedience, which is an acknowledgement of reality.

One of the things Milton was doing in *Paradise Lost* was working out what can be done with the idea of obedience; how, in other words, forbidden pleasures can pervert our sense of hope, and distort the sense we can make out of our hoping. Obedience is, after all, a form of hope. Everything also depends, as Milton shows us in *Paradise Lost*, on what we believe we can and should hope for.

V

'Either criticism is no good at all (a very defensible position),' G. K. Chesterton once wrote, linking literary criticism with criticism in a wider sense, 'or else criticism means saying about an author the very things that would have made him jump out of his boots.' Criticism, in other words – and another word for 'criticism' is 'disobedience' – should have a dramatic effect on the authorities. When Adam and Eve criticized their author, God, it is not clear, and Milton leaves it deliberately ambiguous, whether God jumped out of His boots or not. What they did had an effect on God – it made Him do something rather extraordinary – but it must all have been well within His range, part of His plan, if He was the omnipotent God He claimed to be. Adam and Eve lost all hope and then they found some more in Christ, in His crucifixion and resurrection. But what we do know is that their hope changed: both what they hoped for, and how they did their hoping; put another way, hoping is what they did only after they fell. Before the Fall there was, apparently, nothing to hope for. Their absolute obedience made hoping, made the overcoming or bettering of themselves, something that could never have occurred to them. Their Fall, one could say, brought hope into the world. Obedience circumscribes ambition and desire. At its worst it can pre-empt more than it allows, and allows for. When we live in a state of unconscious obedience we don't think of ourselves as being obedient, we think of ourselves as being realistic, or normal, or reasonable. We live as if we know what life is really like. The most pernicious obedience is the obedience we are unaware of.

If obedience can be a perversion of hope, the cost of an exploitative, absolute dependence, then there must be another kind of hope – normal hope, realistic hope, proper hope – that can be preferred. In his dictionary definition of 'obedience' Johnson cites the following lines from *Paradise Lost*: ' . . . nor can this be, / But by fulfilling that which thou didst want, / Obedience to the Law of God, impos'd / On penaltie of death'; and for 'to obey' he cites, again from *Paradise Lost*: 'Was she thy God, that her thou didst obey, / Before his voice?' It is clear enough from these quotations alone, whether or not one can place them in *Paradise Lost*, what is being illustrated. The wrong kind of obedience produces false hope, the right kind of obedience true hope. The right kind of obedience refers to both whom you obey (God) and how you do your obeying. How you obey can put into question who or what you are obeying: 'that which thou didst want, / Obedience to the Law of God, impos'd' means obedience to God's law was what Adam and Eve really wanted, but it was wanting (absent, in abeyance) when they disobeyed Him. And 'fullfilling that which thou didst want' says, with real hope, that wants can be not simply filled but fulfilled; that wants can be fulfilling, but need to be fulfilled. Real satisfaction is the sign, the consequence, of the right obedience in the right form.

Adam was not obeying God by obeying Eve; and by obeying Eve instead of God he was treating Eve as his (new) God. Obeying Eve 'before' God's 'voice' means both in preference to, and in the presence of, God's voice; so this was clearly a defiance. But there is always the risk that in transferring obediences you might change your object but keep your forms of obedience; or, as was happening in Milton's lifetime, keep your object and change your forms of obedience. You might start treating a person, even a woman, as though she were a God (or for us, though inconceivable to Milton, we might treat our secular commitments as religion by other means; start having, say, a devotional relationship with the environment, or a submissive relation to the law). Or you might start worshipping God without a pope or with a new kind of clergy. But either way it is a question of how and where you obey; and of the fact that obedience can be transferred and transformed. And if that is even possible then obedience is always potentially unstable, even while it claims that it is the very thing that creates stability (just as the fact that people can act (perform) exposes the unpredictability, as well as the fixity, of character). That is to say – and *Paradise Lost* says this, among many other things – obedience always comes with a guarantee (though it is, in fact, a hoped-for, a wished-for, guarantee). And a punishment. You have to believe the promises of the figure you obey (and as promisers go, God has to be the best one ever). But you also have to acknowledge the penalty for disobedience. Obedience involves a promise and a threat. If disobeying Him is the ultimate forbidden act, then obeying Him must be the ultimate unforbidden act. Obedience, as I say, is only an unforbidden pleasure because so much has been forbidden to make it possible.

You must not shock the figure you obey; must not make him jump out of his boots. Rather, you must believe he is unshockable, beyond your provocations. Criticism, if there is to be any, has to be tempered, or disguised. But if the figure you obey is Milton's God, the God of the Judeo-Christian religions, you cannot shock Him because He is omniscient as part of His omnipotence. And if He is omniscient, your disobedience has already been accounted for; it is part of the plan. So you can never be, in His terms, unpredictable, surprising, enigmatic; you can never be ahead of the game because you *are* the game. So the famous opening lines of Milton's poem announce a paradox by telling a familiar story:

> *Of Man's First Disobedience, and the Fruit*
> *Of that Forbidden Tree, whose mortal taste*
> *Brought Death into the World, and all our woe,*
> *With loss of Eden, till one greater Man*
> *Restore us, and regain the blissful Seat,*
> *Sing Heav'nly Muse . . .*

It is extraordinary to imagine our first disobedience; so familiar are we in our fallen state with our disobedience it has become second nature. We can't remember the first time we were disobedient, let alone easily imagine, as Genesis does for us, the very first disobedience ever, the primal scene of disobedience. And it is difficult to understand in our fallen minds quite what obedience meant to Adam and Eve before they had been disobedient. And we presume in our fallen state that they really knew nothing about obedience until they were disobedient, or certainly not enough about it. They might, for example, have thought that obedience was a state of temptation, or permanent anticipation, or essential ignorance. But all such speculation is just that, speculation, because there is no going back to how we used to think, if thinking, indeed, was what Adam and Eve ever did. We need, in other words, to bear in mind Stanley Fish's salutary injunction in his all too aptly entitled *Surprised by Sin*: '*Paradise Lost* is a poem about how its readers came to be the way they are; its method . . . is to provoke in its readers wayward, fallen responses which are then corrected by one of several authoritative voices (the narrator, God, Raphael, Michael, the Son).' The first disobedience, though, as Milton tells us at the outset, was one that bore mixed fruits: death, and 'all our woe' (which is a lot); and Christ the redeeming son (who is even more). No Fall, no Christ, no Christianity, no *Paradise Lost*. The fruit of this first disobedience is that we were left always hoping for something better; this first disobedience was inspired by the wrong kind of hope – for forbidden knowledge – but one of the consequences of the wrong kind of hope was that we could then have the right kind of hope once we had seen our error. This is effectively what Michael tells Adam towards the end of the final book of *Paradise Lost*, as cited by Johnson for his definition of 'obedience':

> . . . *hee, who comes thy Saviour, shall recure,*
> *Not by destroying Satan, but his works*
> *In thee and in thy Seed: nor can this be,*
> *But by fulfilling that which thou didst want,*
> *Obedience to the Law of God, impos'd*
> *On penaltie of death, and suffering death,*
> *The penaltie to thy transgression due,*
> *And due to theirs which out of thine will grow:*
> *So onely can high Justice rest appaid.*

Christ will 'recure' them, though there is a strange ambiguity here that suggests that Adam and Eve were originally cured of something, and needed recuring; as though there could have been something wrong with them more original than original sin. Or at least Milton allows us to wonder about this (the *Oxford English Dictionary* has for 'recure' simply 'to cure', clearly Milton's primary sense, but Milton would have known that the Latinate prefix 're' meant 'again'). If there is an ambiguity here we might just say that Milton wants us to think about what, if anything, Adam and Eve might have been suffering from in the Garden of Eden; as if he couldn't quite imagine a life without suffering; as though unforbidden pleasures couldn't be exempt from it. But, anyway, 'high Justice' can only be 'appaid' (that is, satisfied) by their dire punishment and their renewed (because recovered) aspiration, 'Obedience to the Law of God.' Everything going according to plan, the forbidden, transgression, the first disobedience, can lead us back to the unforbidden, our 'blissful Seat'. Disobedience makes us really appreciate obedience. You have got to be cruel to be kind. So, at least, God seems to think (in fact you've only got to be kind to be kind). 'The reason why the poem is so good,' the poet-critic William Empson famously remarked in *Milton's God*, 'is that it makes God so bad.'

But for my purposes, in this chapter, I want to suggest that whatever else Milton is doing here he is making us think about what unforbidden pleasures might be like when we attempt to recover them, and especially when we attempt to recover them having tasted the forbidden pleasures they always coexisted with. This is because what I am interested in is the recovery of unforbidden pleasures, or their renewal, following the experience of the forbidden. And, above all, I am interested in the way in which – in Genesis, in *Paradise Lost* – unforbidden pleasures only really exist, only come to consciousness, as unforbidden after the experience of the forbidden. Clearly only adults, not infants, are capable of unforbidden pleasures in the light of their experience of forbidden pleasures. At its most minimal, Milton shows us in *Paradise Lost*, you find out something new, something else, after an act of disobedience (you know something new about sovereignty after you cut off a king's head; and part of what you may then want to know is what, if anything, you want to recover from the time before the fateful, 'first' disobedience). Before disobedience, obedience; though it may be unwitting obedience, it may not be experienced as obedience, or obedience may not be experienced as a problem. But after disobedience there can only be faux innocence (the disobedience can only be punished but not undone, which tells us something about the despair inherent in punishment). You only find out what your obedience entails, what it has been costing you, when you are disobedient. It is not that rules are made to be broken, but that you find out what the rules are made of in the breaking of them, as well as what you are made of. Adam and Eve had a better idea of what they were up against – or rather, of what they and their God were like – through the Fall. And that must have been something God wanted. Obedience is the wish not to know something. Obedience is the wish to stop time; obedience stops us growing by making us remember the rules (God is the name no one can afford to forget). And obedience is what is always required.

Milton, Johnson wrote in his *Life of Milton* (1779),

> hated monarchs in the state and prelates in the church; for he hated all whom he was required to obey. It is to be suspected that his predominant desire was to destroy rather than establish, and that he felt not so much the love of liberty as repugnance to authority.

Yet Milton, who in Johnson's words, 'hated all whom he was required to obey', wrote a poem about how and why we are all required to obey. And he drew a remarkable distinction from Johnson: Milton, 'felt not so much the love of liberty as repugnance to authority'. It would be truer to say that Milton felt repugnance to certain forms of authority, but it would be infinitely less interesting. It is more interesting to wonder what a repugnance to authority might involve; and how it could come about that a repugnance to authority could be more important than a love of liberty – could, indeed, displace it so that one's hatred of authority could lead one to forget one's love of liberty; as if one could be bewitched by that hatred, and could forget the point of it. The forbidden always incites our hatred, and can seduce us into forgetting about our love of liberty. We take liberties in an attempt to recover our love of freedom. Only in our unforbidden pleasures do we love our liberty without needing a repugnance to authority. Believing in the forbidden is believing in the authorities. In our unforbidden pleasures we get a glimpse of what a life without obedience would be like. A life in which pleasure and terror were no longer inextricable.

VI

When the psychoanalyst Jonathan Lear describes, in his essay 'The Call of Another's Words', people for whom it 'is not a concern that they fall short of a now impossible ideal; it is a concern that there is no longer an ideal to fall short of', he is talking of the fear of there being nothing or no one worth obeying. So we must talk then both of the fear of disobedience, and the fear of having nothing or no one to obey; and of what requires our obedience as opposed to our engagement; of what, in Rowan Williams's terms, invites us to argue, and what forces us to submit. There are certain arguments we can't afford not to have. And other arguments we need not have at all.

We don't, for example, tend to describe all rule-bound behaviour as obedience. We don't think of ourselves as being obedient to the rules of a game, say, but of the rules making the game possible. We may think of schools, or religious orders, or prisons, or even families as requiring obedience, but not skating rinks, or supermarkets, or poetry readings. Obedience becomes an issue, or the issue, when something about following a rule – something about the rule itself, or something about how the rule has to be followed – is troubling. Obedience is invoked when dissent is predicted, when the authorities themselves – the rule-setters – already know there is a problem: they have made a rule that people are going to be tempted to break. So those who demand obedience have already imagined for themselves why it may not be forthcoming. They have imagined, that is to say, the very real pleasures of breaking the rule. They are taking a kind of risk that might involve, for example, some conscious or unconscious complicity with those who refuse to abide by their rules. Officially they know where they stand; unofficially they are double agents. They know that one thing they are doing with their rule is tantalizing those who must abide by it.

If, in Rowan Williams's words quoted earlier, the good is something we argue about, the good cannot be something that requires our obedience. It requires, rather, our arguing ('the idea,' William Empson writes in *Milton's God*, against Milton's God and his many devotees, 'that there actually couldn't be a moral debate in a literary work amounts to a collapse of the Western mind'). Obedience wants to put a stop to the argument, to pre-empt the debate. Freud, with his 'method' of free association, wants to take the debate for granted, as it were. Freud says: the argument is always already going on (in oneself, and between oneself and various other people, both real and imaginary); the question is whether we can create the conditions in which we want to hear it, and hear about it; whether we can make a compelling case for the argument, rather than for its suppression. His conditions are the psychoanalytic setting, with its two explicit demands: say whatever comes into your head; and pay for the treatment. 'The fundamental technical rule of this procedure of "free association",' Freud writes in his 'Two Encyclopaedia Articles' of 1923, means that:

The treatment is begun by the patient being required
to put himself in the position of an attentive and dispas-
sionate self-observer, merely to read off all the time the
surface of his consciousness, and on the one hand to make
a duty of the most complete honesty while on the other
hand not to hold back any idea from communication,
even if (1) he feels that it is too disagreeable or if (2) he
judges that it is nonsensical or (3) too unimportant or
(4) irrelevant to what is being looked for. It is uniformly
found that precisely those ideas which provoke these
last-mentioned reactions are of particular value in discovering the forgotten material.

The preconditions for doing psychoanalysis – for taking up what Jacques Lacan rightly calls the 'psychoanalytic
opportunity' – are the following of this rule, as far as is
possible. Unlike the confessional, in which the person
always already knows what he must disclose, the analytic
patient cannot know beforehand what he has to say. Unlike
a man on trial, the analytic patient has only, as it were, a
superficial sense of what he is and isn't guilty of. The analyst aims for a recure, to use Milton's word; the analyst
aims to cure the patient, as the psychoanalyst Masud Khan
put it, of his already established self-cure, because the
patient is deemed to be suffering now from the self-cure of

his organized symptoms. He has come to conclusions about himself that are inconclusive.

The difference between consenting to free associate and obeying God's laws is that through free association the patient can discover what has been forbidden him, and so what he has forbidden himself, because he has repressed this knowledge; and what all this might have cost him in terms of inhibition, and in terms of uncompleted actions (as well as the actions of speaking and thinking and feeling and desiring). Then, perhaps, the patient can make some choices; choices about which rules he believes are worth following, and which rules he has merely been following, consciously or unconsciously, for fear of punishment (the aim of the analysis, the analyst Roger Money-Kyrle once remarked, is to prove the irrelevance of the inhibition). The devout believer in God's laws, on the other hand, always already knows what is forbidden her, and has no choice in the matter (she has her reasons ready to hand: she remembers them). For the so-called analytic patient, the good is to be argued about; for the believer, the good has already been decided. The psychoanalytic patient is, in other words, Kant's self-legislating individual: not a law unto himself, but a person who can argue, with himself and with other people, about what the laws should be, about which rules are of value, and why. He is a person who can give and hear reasons.

All you must do, Freud says, is notice the disagreeable, the nonsensical, the unimportant and the irrelevant, and voice it, to a psychoanalyst, who can respond and not respond in a certain way (and, by implication, then you can recover an appetite to speak with greater freedom to other people, and to yourself – as if to say: we should be more attentive to the affinities between people who have little in common; which would include the affinities we have with our selves). The criteria for censorship could not be more ordinary – no qualifications are required to discern them, no learning, no mysterious talents; and what you can discover is what Freud calls 'the forgotten material', the unconscious after-effects of your conscious and unconscious obedience. The analytic patient discovers he is the casualty of forgotten obediences. Some, at least, of his forbidden pleasures will be revealed as unforbidden pleasures after all. Other of the forbidden pleasures can be redescribed (debated, argued about). And some of the forbidden pleasures will remain forbidden because they are the preconditions for our preferred story about ourselves. But most importantly, the unforbidden will have recovered its allure. And some versions of the forbidden will be reopened.

We inhibit ourselves through self-criticism, through obedience to our own largely unconscious rules. We are forbidden, and we forbid ourselves, a certain freedom of thought and feeling and desire and speech. And then we turn this ferocious, unrelenting self-criticism into an unforbidden pleasure. It is, as Milton makes clear, second nature for us to be obedient. But we should notice that it is, of course, by definition, unforbidden to obey the forbidders. There are, in other words, unforbidden pleasures of which we should be duly suspicious. And other, infinitely more various, unforbidden pleasures that we might enjoy, once the forbidders become people we can argue with. We can begin to enjoy our unforbidden pleasures and our forbidden pleasures anew only when we can dispel the curse of our obscene, inordinate self-criticism. We need to be able to argue with, and let others argue with, whatever is most forbidding about ourselves. What begins as obedience ends as self-criticism.

Against Self-Criticism

All silencing of discussion is an assumption of infallibility.

John Stuart Mill, *On Liberty*

I

Jacques Lacan famously remarked that there must surely be something ironic about Christ's injunction to love thy neighbour as thyself, because actually people hate themselves. Indeed, it seemed rather as if, given the way people treat each other, they had always loved their neighbours in the way they loved themselves. That is, with a good deal of cruelty and disregard. 'After all,' Lacan wrote in *Four Fundamental Concepts of Psychoanalysis*, 'the people who followed Christ were not so brilliant.' Lacan, at this moment in his talk, is of course implicitly comparing Freud with Christ, many of whose followers in Lacan's view had betrayed Freud's vision. And that meant, simply, that they had read him in the wrong way. There had been a failure of literary criticism – literary criticism being notably a phrase, and a practice, that has had rather more staying power than the idea of literary appreciation (literary appreciation, with its Paterian associations, has a whiff of the effete, whereas criticism always implies something more determinedly robust and intelligent). In broaching the possibility of being, in some way, against self-criticism, we have to imagine a world in which celebration is less suspect than criticism; in which the alternatives of celebration and criticism are seen as a determined narrowing of the repertoire; and in which we praise whatever we can.

Lacan's comparison, which he immediately qualifies – 'Freud was not Christ, but he was perhaps something like Viridiana' (the eponymous character in Luis Buñuel's film, who is a corrupted nun) – is itself a suggestive interpretation of at least this one element in Christianity. Lacan could be understood to be saying here that, from a Freudian point of view, Christ's story about love was a cover story: a repression of, and a self-cure for, ambivalence. In Freud's vision of things we are, above all, ambivalent animals: wherever we hate, we love; wherever we love, we hate. If someone can satisfy us, they can also frustrate us; and if someone can frustrate us, we always believe that they can satisfy us. We criticize when we are frustrated – or when we are trying to describe our frustration, however obliquely – and praise when we are more satisfied, and vice versa. Ambivalence does not, in the Freudian story, mean mixed feelings, it means opposing feelings. 'Ambivalence has to be distinguished from having mixed feelings about someone,' Charles Rycroft writes, in his appropriately entitled *A Critical Dictionary of Psychoanalysis* (as though an 'Uncritical' dictionary would be somehow simple-minded):

> It refers to an underlying emotional attitude in which the contradictory attitudes derive from a common source and are interdependent, whereas mixed feelings may be based on a realistic assessment of the imperfect nature of the object.

Love and hate – a too simple, or too familiar, vocabulary, and so never quite the right names for what we might want to say – are the common source, the elemental feelings with which we apprehend the world; and they are interdependent in the sense that you can't have one without the other, and that they mutually inform each other. The way we hate people depends on the way we love them, and vice versa. And given that these contradictory feelings are our 'common source' they enter into everything we do. They are the medium in which we do everything. We are ambivalent, in Freud's view, about anything and everything that matters to us; indeed, ambivalence is the way we recognize that someone or something has become significant to us. This means that we are ambivalent about ambivalence (and the forbidden, we should remember, is an object of desire, which is why it is forbidden), about love and hate and sex and each other and ourselves, and so on. Wherever there is an object of desire, in this account, there is ambivalence. But Freud's insistence about our ambivalence, about us as fundamentally ambivalent animals, is also his way of saying that we are never quite as obedient as we seem to be: that where there is devotion there is always protest; that where there is trust there is suspicion; and that where there is self-hatred (guilt) there is self-love. We may not be able to imagine a life in which we don't spend a large amount of our time criticizing ourselves and others; but we should keep in mind the self-love that is always in play.

We are never as good as we should be; and neither, it seems, are other people. Indeed, a life without a so-called critical faculty would seem an idiocy, though quite what kind of idiocy is not entirely clear. What are we, after all, but our powers of discrimination, our taste, the violence of our preferences? Our insufficiency is patent (though we do need to bear in mind that to feel not good enough is to have already consented to the standard we are being judged by). Clearly, self-criticism, and the self as critical, are essential to our sense, our picture, of our so-called selves. 'It often happens,' Swift wrote, 'that if a lie be believed only for an hour, it hath done its work, and there is no farther occasion for it' (*Examiner*, No. XIV, 1710). The lie that self-criticism can so easily be – the relentless misnaming of the self – seems to require endless reiteration, like the propaganda that it is.

And, by the same token, nothing makes us more critical, more confounded – more suspicious, or appalled, or even mildly amused – than the suggestion that we should drop all this relentless criticism; that we should be less impressed by it. Or at least that self-criticism should cease to have the hold over us that it does. One reason, for example, that we might be less impressed, less in awe, of the part of ourselves that criticizes ourselves, is that there is one very striking fact about it, which I will come back to. The self-critical part of ourselves – which Freud calls the 'superego' – is remarkably narrow-minded; it has an unusually impoverished vocabulary; and it is, like all propagandists, relentlessly repetitive. It is cruelly intimidating – Lacan writes of 'the obscene superego' – and it never brings us any news about ourselves. There are only ever two or three things we endlessly accuse ourselves of, and they are all too familiar; a stuck record, as we say, but in both senses – the superego is reiterative. The stuck record of the past, it never surprises us ('something there badly not wrong', Samuel Beckett's line from *Worstward Ho*, is exactly what it must not say). It is, in short, strikingly unimaginative; both about morality and about our selves – the selves it insists on diminishing. Were we to meet this figure socially, as it were, this accusatory character, this internal critic, we would think there was something wrong with him. He would just be boring and cruel. We might think that something terrible had happened to him. That he was living in the aftermath, in the fallout of some catastrophe. And we would be right.

II

Hamlet, we should remember, wanted to 'catch the conscience of the king', and thought the 'play' was where it could be caught – 'The play's the thing / Wherein I'll catch the conscience of the king'. For 'catch' the *OED* has: 'to seize or take hold of, to ensnare, to deceive, to surprise . . . to take, to intercept . . . to seize by the senses or intellect, to apprehend'; it also had, in the sixteenth century, our modern connotation of 'to catch out', but the term derives originally from hunting and fishing. Clearly it would be a very revealing, perhaps overexposing, thing to be able to do, to have been able to catch the conscience of a or the king (and especially, perhaps, in 1604, when James I's kingship was in question); conscience did not then have simply or solely our more modern sense of some kind of internal moral regulation but also meant 'inward knowledge or consciousness'; the dictionary has, for 1611, 'inmost thought, mind, heart'. To catch the conscience of a king would be to radically expose his most private preoccupations and, in the words of the dictionary, it would be to expose 'the faculty or principle which pronounces upon the moral quality of one's actions or motives'. These definitions are interesting not least because they raise the question of just how private or inmost or intimate conscience is supposed to be. And questions about what we should want to know about a king, or indeed about any authoritative voice (about, say, James I, and what his religious affiliations might entail). We might wonder, for example, whether conscience itself has a conscience, and so on. Morality, one might think – not to mention the religion of state that the king represented – would have to be public. And yet these definitions contemporary with *Hamlet* intimate that one's morality might also be the most private thing about oneself – private from the authorities, given that the language of morality was the language of religion, and *Hamlet* was written at a time of considerable religious divisions; but also, perhaps, private in the sense of hidden from the self.

One might carry a morality, live as if a certain morality were true, without quite knowing what it was. It would be like a morality that had no texts to refer to; nor even knew, perhaps, that reference was required. It could be like certain versions of Protestantism (the inner light is not a reading light). And at its most extreme the 'faculty or principle which pronounces upon the moral quality of one's actions or motives' might have no discernible or remotely popular cultural moorings. So in speaking one's mind one might be speaking all sorts of other minds, some recognizable, some not. Hamlet, Brian Cummings writes in *Mortal Thoughts*, 'far from speaking his mind, confronts us with a fragmentary repository of alternative selves, and searches within for the limits of being'. Once we have the idea of alternative selves, we will have questions about the limits of being, about what or who we can take ourselves to be. If conscience can be caught – like a fish, like a criminal – it might become part of that fragmentary repository of alternative selves that resembles a troupe of actors. If the play is the thing, then we can say that it was useful to have a cultural form in which the conscience of a king – or indeed of anyone; conscience itself being like a king – could be caught, exposed, seen to be like a character. And therefore thought about, and discussed and argued with. What does the conscience of the king look like? Who, or what, does it remind us of? Being able to reflect on one's conscience – being able to look at the voice of conscience from varying points of view – is itself a radical act (and one that psychoanalysis would turn into a formal treatment). After all, if the voice of conscience is not to be obeyed, what is to be done with it?

Freud, it is worth remembering, used *Hamlet* in *The Interpretation of Dreams* (1900) as, among other things, a way of understanding the obscene severities of conscience (he hadn't coined the term 'superego' in 1900: he first used it in *The Ego and the Id* in 1923). In what seems, in retrospect, a rather simple picture of a person, Freud proposed that we were driven by quickly acculturated biological instincts, tempered by controls and prohibitions internalized from the culture through our parents. Conscience, which Freud would later incorporate into his notion of the superego, was there to protect and prohibit the individual from desires that endangered him, or were presumed to. In Freud's view, we have conscience so that we may not perish of the truth – the truth, that is, of our desire. *Hamlet*

92

was unusually illuminating for Freud because it showed him how conscience worked; and how psychoanalytic interpretation worked; and how psychoanalysis could itself become part of the voice of conscience. It showed too that conscience was voracious in its recruitments. 'The loathing which should drive [Hamlet] on to revenge,' Freud wrote, 'is replaced in him by self-reproaches, by scruples of conscience, which remind him that he himself is literally no better than the sinner whom he is to punish.' Hamlet, in Freud's view, turns the murderous aggression he feels towards Claudius against himself; conscience is the consequence of uncompleted revenge. Originally there were other people we wanted to murder; but this was too dangerous so we murder ourselves through self-reproach, and we murder ourselves to punish ourselves for having such murderous thoughts. And we have to be clear about this: Freud is using *Hamlet* to say that conscience is a form of character assassination, the character assassination of everyday life. We are continually, if unconsciously, mutilating and deforming our own character. Indeed, so unrelenting is this internal violence that we have no idea what we are like without it. We know virtually nothing about ourselves because we judge ourselves before we have a chance to see ourselves (as though in panic). Or, to put it differently, we can judge only what we recognize ourselves as able to judge. What can't be judged can't be seen. What happens to everything that is not subject to approval or disapproval, to everything that we have not been taught how to judge?

Freud's way of formulating this shows us how conscience obscures self-knowledge, and he intimates that this may be its primary function; that the judged self can only be judged but not known; and that guilt hides the self in the guise of exposing it. This then allows us to think that it is complicitous not to stand up to, not to contest, this internal tyranny by what is only one part – a small but loud part – of the self. So frightened are we by the superego that we identify with it, we speak on its behalf, to avoid antagonizing it (complicity is delegated bullying). Tragedy is the genre that shows us what is at stake in contesting and abiding by conscience, and its related terms. So in this play, or rather, in one way of seeing this play, Hamlet is arguing with his own and other people's consciences, with unique eloquence and subtlety.

Hamlet, Freud intimated, has such complex self-rumination and such relentless self-accusation – the two becoming virtually synonymous, the so-called internal world being among other things an ongoing revenge tragedy – because of the violence he has been unable to enact. The drama is internalized. Hamlet's battling with his conscience – not the voice of conscience alone but the voices called up in Hamlet to contest it – is the drama of the play. So Hamlet, we should notice, is a genius of self-reproach, because of the dialogues with his conscience that he can engage in. In this play – and in this sense literature might be the thing to catch the conscience – the dialogues around and about self-criticism seem like one of the most imaginative things we can do. Hamlet captures our imagination because of what has captured his imagination, and the ways in which it has captured his imagination. It is the links between self-criticism and what Brian Cummings called the 'limits of being' that Shakespeare dramatizes in *Hamlet*. Indeed, it is only because our consciences are as they are – are the kind of artefact we have made for ourselves – that there is such a thing as tragedy at all. Tragedy, one could say, is the cultural form in which we have been trying to reveal something not about the real horror of life, but about the horror of life lived under the aegis of a certain kind of conscience. Self-criticism is nothing if it is not the defining, and usually the overdefining, of the limits of being. But, ironically, if that's the right word, the limits of being are announced and enforced before so-called being has had much of a chance to speak for itself. The Freudian superego is the limit that forbids you to discover your own limits. It is pre-emptive in its restrictiveness. Hamlet's conversation with himself and others about conscience allows him to speak in ways no one had quite spoken before.

It is, then, of some interest that Freud chose *Hamlet* to start really thinking about conscience, and that thinking about conscience requires thinking about tragedy. There is, it dawned on Freud, something we may need to be freed from. After interpreting Hamlet's apparent procrastinations in the play with the new-found authority of the new-found psychoanalyst, Freud then needed to add something by way of qualification that was at once itself a loophole and a limit. 'But just as all neurotic symptoms,' he wrote,

> and, for that matter, dreams are capable of being 'over-interpreted', and indeed need to be, if they are to be fully understood, so all genuinely creative writings are the product of more than a single impulse in the poet's mind, and are open to more than a single interpretation.

It is as though Freud's guilt about his own aggression in asserting his interpretation of what he calls the 'deepest layers' in *Hamlet* – his claim to sovereignty over the text and the character of Hamlet – leads him to open up the play, having closed it down (the Freudian superego always has a sovereign interpretation of our behaviour; we consent to the superego's interpretation; we believe our self-reproaches are true; we are overimpressed without noticing that that is what we are being). You can only understand anything that matters – dreams, neurotic symptoms, literature – by overinterpreting it; by seeing it from different aspects as the product of multiple impulses. Overinterpretation here means not settling for one interpretation, however apparently compelling it is. Indeed, the implication is – and here is Freud's ongoing suspicion, or ambivalence, about psychoanalysis – that the more persuasive, the more compelling, the more authoritative, the interpretation is, the less credible it is, or should be. The interpretation might be the violent attempt to presume to set a limit where no limit can be set (if one interpretation 'explained' *Hamlet* we wouldn't need *Hamlet* any more: *Hamlet* as a play would have been murdered). Authority wants to replace the world with itself. Overinterpretation means not being stopped in your tracks by what you are most persuaded by; it means assuming that to believe one interpretation is to radically misunderstand the object one is interpreting, and indeed interpretation itself.

Tragic heroes always underinterpret, are always emperors of one idea. And the tragic hero is always the enemy of what Freud calls, and calls for – overinterpretation. Hamlet, we could say, is a great overinterpreter of his experience; and it is this – the sheer range and complexity of his thoughts; his interest in his thought from different aspects – that makes him such an unusual so-called tragic hero, and that gives *Hamlet*, I think, its unique status. 'Emerson was distinguished,' George Santayana wrote, 'not by what he knew but by the number of ways he had of knowing it.' Freud was beginning to fear, at this moment in *The Interpretation of Dreams*, when he was writing about *Hamlet* – and rightly, as it turned out – that psychoanalysis could be undistinguished if it had only one way of knowing what it thought it knew. It was dawning on him, prompted by his reading of *Hamlet*, that psychoanalysis, at its worst, could be a method of underinterpretation. And to take that seriously was to take the limits of psychoanalysis seriously; and indeed the limits of any description of human nature that organizes itself around one essential metaphor. The Oedipus complex – a story about the paramount significance of forbidden desire in the individual's development – was the essential psychoanalytic metaphor. Comparing *Hamlet* with the psychoanalytic readings of *Hamlet* as an Oedipal crisis would soon more than confirm Freud's misgivings about the uses and misuses of psychoanalysis. Indeed, it confirms Gilles Deleuze and Felix Guattari's point in *Anti-Oedipus* that the function of the Oedipus myth in psychoanalysis is, paradoxically, to restore law and order; to contain within a culturally prestigious classical myth the unpredictable, prodigal desires that Freud had broached, and which psychoanalysis threatened to unleash.

So there is Cummings's distinction between the notion of Hamlet speaking his mind as opposed to his speaking a 'fragmentary repository of alternative selves'; and there is Freud's authoritative psychoanalytic interpretation of Hamlet highly qualified by his subsequent promotion of 'overinterpretation'; and Shakespeare's and Hamlet's troupe of actors who will perform a play that will be the thing to catch the conscience of a king. And there is of course Hamlet's question in the famous soliloquy in which he tells us something about suicide, and something about death, and something about all the unknown and unknowable future experiences that death also represents. And he does this by telling us something about conscience. Or, rather, two things about conscience.

The first quarto of *Hamlet* has, 'Thus conscience does make cowards of us all,' while the second quarto has, 'Thus conscience does make cowards.' If conscience makes cowards of us all, then we are all in the same boat; this is just the way it is. If conscience simply makes cowards we can more easily wonder what else it might be able to make. Either way, and they are clearly different, conscience makes something of us; it is a maker, if not of selves, then of something about selves. It is an internal artist, of a kind. Freud will say that the superego – which, as we shall see, is both similar to and different from conscience – is something we make, which then, in turn, makes us into something, into certain kinds of people (just as, say, Frankenstein's monster makes Frankenstein into something that he wasn't before he made the monster). The superego, I will say, after Freud, casts us as certain kinds of character: it, as it were, tells us who we really are. It is an essentialist: it claims to know us in a way that no one else, including ourselves, can ever do. And, like a mad god, it is omniscient: it behaves as if it can predict the future by claiming to know the consequences of our actions (when we know, in a more imaginative part of ourselves, that most actions are morally equivocal, and change over time in our estimation; no apparently self-destructive act is ever only self-destructive; no good is purely and simply that). The superego is the sovereign interpreter, and it forbids what Freud calls, usefully, 'overinterpretation', the word making us wonder what the standard of proper or sufficient interpretation might be if this (psychoanalytic reading) is overinterpretation, and over-interpretation is required. What is the norm, and what kind of norm is it, if this excess is necessary? The superego tells us what we take to be the truth about ourselves. Self-criticism, that is to say, is an unforbidden pleasure. We seem to relish the way it makes us suffer. It gives, and has given, unforbidden pleasure a bad name. Unforbidden pleasures are always the pleasures we don't particularly want to think about; we just implicitly take it for granted that each day will bring its necessary quotient of self-disappointment. That every day we will fail to be as good as we should be; but without our being given the resources, the language, to wonder who or what is setting the pace; or where these rather punishing standards come from. How can we find out what we think of all this when conscience never lets go?

The new Arden *Hamlet* glosses 'conscience': 'some commentators argue that conscience means "introspection" here rather than a sense of morality . . . Certainly the context indicates that Hamlet means "fear of punishment after death" rather than "innate sense of good and bad".' The ambiguity, as I have said, between conscience as inner mentation as opposed to conscience as inner morality is integral to the matter at hand. The question is whether there is more to our inner worlds than our sense, innate or otherwise, of good and bad. Or indeed, whether there are multiple, or competing, or largely unconscious, moralities that we live by unwittingly. *Hamlet* makes us wonder: if conscience makes us cowards, what is conscience like? Cowardice, after all, may be, as the dictionary puts it, the 'display . . . of ignoble fear in the face of pain, danger or difficulty', a coward being a 'pusillanimous person', someone 'wanting firmness of mind . . . mean-spirited' in Chambers modern dictionary. Cowardice is deemed to be unimpressive, inappropriate, shameful fear. We are cowardly when we are not at our best, or as we should be, when frightened. There are, in other words, acceptable and unacceptable versions of fearfulness; and this means we should be fearful in certain ways, and fearful of certain objects. Fear, like everything else, is subject to cultural norms. So if conscience makes cowards, it demeans us; it is the part of ourselves that humiliates us, that makes us, in that horrifying phrase, ashamed of ourselves. But what if it makes the very selves that it encourages us to be ashamed of? What if it makes us into humiliatable objects by always underinterpreting, by being so starkly narrow-minded? As Hamlet famously tells us, sometimes conscience torments us by stopping us killing ourselves when our lives are actually unbearable. It can, as Hamlet can't quite say, be a kind of torturer; even making us go on living when we know, in a more imaginative part of ourselves, that our lives have become intolerable. Conscience, that is to say, can seduce us into betraying ourselves. Indeed, in Freud's figure of the superego, as we shall see, it is the part of our mind that makes us lose our minds; the moralist that prevents us from evolving a personal, more complex and subtle morality; that prevents us from finding, by experiment, what may be the limits of our being. So when Richard III says, in the final act of his own play, 'O coward conscience, how dost thou afflict me!', a radical alternative is being proposed. That conscience makes cowards of us all because it is itself cowardly. We believe in, we identify with, this starkly condemnatory and punitively forbidding part of ourselves; and yet this supposedly authoritative part of ourselves is itself a coward.

We are afflicted with its cowardice. Conscience is intimidating because it is intimidated. What, we might wonder – and this was to be Freud's question – is our conscience intimidated by if it is not intimidated by God? And how is it, and why is it, that morality as we have conceived of it is born of intimidation? What other kind of morality might there be? If it is, as Richard says, 'coward conscience' then we might be fearing the wrong objects in the wrong way. If we have been living by a forbidding morality, what would an unforbidding morality look like? We have to imagine not that we are cowardly, but that we have been living by the morality of a coward. So this too we need to consider: that the ferocity of our conscience might be a form of cowardice. Clearly there are moralities inspired by fear, but what would a morality be, or be like, that was inspired by desire? It would, as Hamlet's great soliloquy perhaps suggests, be a morality, a conscience, that had a different relation to the unknown. The coward, after all, always thinks he knows what he fears, and knows that he doesn't have the wherewithal to deal with it. The coward, like Freud's superego, is too knowing. A coward – or rather, the cowardly part of ourselves – is like a person who must not have a new experience (a character in one of Norman Mailer's novels says, 'you learn everything fighting your fear': conscience says, this is a fear you can't fight). Hamlet is talking about suicide, but talking about suicide is a way of talking about experiences one has really never had before.

> Who would fardels bear,
> To grunt and sweat under a weary life,
> But that the dread of something after death,
> The undiscovered country from whose bourn
> No traveller returns, puzzles the will
> And makes us rather bear those ills we have
> Than fly to others that we know not of?
> Thus conscience does make cowards –
> And thus the native hue of resolution
> Is sicklied o'er with the pale cast of thought,
> And enterprises of great pith and moment

With this regard their currents turn awry,
And lose the name of action.

'The undiscovered country from whose bourn / No trav-
eller returns' is also the unknown and unknowable future,
'bourn' reminding us that our relation to the future is also
a continual 'being born', as well as something we have to
find ways of bearing. One of the ways we bear the
unknownness of the future is to treat it as though it was,
in fact, the past; and as though the past was something we
did know about (Freud would formalize this idea in his
concept of transference; we invent new people on the basis
of past familial relationships: as if we really knew those
people and could use that knowledge as a reliable guide).
This fear of death, and of the unknowable future – the fear
that it will be, one way or another, only punishing, as our
conscience instructs us – makes us cowards. There is, we
should note, in this so-called melancholia no expectation
that the unknown will be either better than expected, or
wholly other than the way it can be imagined. 'The native
hue of resolution', something perhaps more innate (the
dictionary has, 'natural to a person'), is then 'sicklied o'er
with the pale cast of thought'. As if to say, thinking like
this – thinking as conscience makes us think – is like an
illness; if there is a pale cast of thought, there must be or

could be a bright, or brilliant, or full-blooded cast of thought; 'cast of thought' reminding us of the cast of a play, and that thoughts might be cast like actors are cast; thoughts in role, thoughts as playing parts, thoughts as scripted. Conscience as scripted can never be out of character; and we may never be quite able to work out who wrote the script. It is likely, in the context, and in the moment of the play, that Hamlet, as the Arden editors Anne Thompson and Neil Taylor say, is talking about fear of punishment after death; the life after death as conceived by the contested Christianities that Shakespeare inhabited. But Hamlet is also talking about, in the context of this play – a play acutely self-conscious about its own theatricality – how conscience feeds us our lines, and whether, indeed, conscience feeds us our best lines; especially given its pale cast of thought.

Talking about conscience though – and, of course, the prospect of death – gives Hamlet some of his best lines. If conscience doesn't feed us our best lines, Hamlet at least suggests, talking and writing about conscience might. Conscience, in its all too impoverished vocabulary and its all too serious and suffocating drama, needs to be over-interpreted. Underinterpreted it can only be taken on its own terms as propaganda (the superego speaks only propaganda about the self, which is why it is so boring, and yet so easy to listen to). Psychoanalysis was to be about whether the superego – not conscience, but akin to it – could be changed through redescription. Something as unrelenting as our internal soliloquys of self-reproach, Freud realized, necessitated unusually imaginative redescriptions. Without such redescriptions – and *Hamlet* is of course one – what Cummings calls the 'fragmentary repository of alternative selves' will be silenced. The slings and arrows of outrageous fortune are as nothing compared with the murderous mufflings and insinuations and distortions of the superego. Because it is the project of the superego, as conceived of by Freud, to render the individual utterly solipsistic, incapable of exchange: so self-mortified, so loathsome, so inadequate, so isolated, so self-obsessed, so boring and bored, so guilty that no one could possibly love or desire them. The solitary modern individual and his Freudian superego, a slave and a master in a world of their own. 'What do I fear?' Richard III asks at the end of his play; 'Myself? There's none else by.'

III

Like all unforbidden pleasures, self-criticism, or self-reproach, is always available and accessible. What needs to be understood is: why is it unforbidden, and why is it a pleasure? And, following on from this, how has it come about that we are so bewitched by our self-hatred, so impressed and credulous in the face of our self-criticism, as unimaginative as it usually is? And why is it akin to a judgement without a jury? A jury, after all, represents some kind of consensus as an alternative to autocracy (when Algernon Sidney wrote in his posthumously published 1698 *Discourses Concerning Government* that 'the strength of every judgment consists in the verdict of these juries, which the judges do not give, but pronounce or declare', he was making the figure of a judge a spokesperson for a diversity of voices, not a sovereign authority). I want to suggest that guilt – apparently legitimated self-hatred – can also be a refuge. That we need to be able to tell the difference between useful forms of responsibility taken for acts committed, and the evasions of self-contempt (shame is as much about being exposed as about what is exposed). An orgy of self-criticism is always preferable to the other, more daunting, more pleasurable, engagements (or arguments: this doesn't mean that no one is ever culpable; it means that culpability will always be more complicated than it looks; guilt is always underinterpreted). And that self-criticism, when it isn't useful in the way any self-correcting approach can be, is self-hypnosis.

It is judgement as spell, or curse, not as conversation; it is an order, not a negotiation; it is dogma, not overinterpretation. Psychoanalysis, that is to say, sets itself the task of wanting to have a conversation with someone who, because he knows what a conversation is, is determinedly never going to have one. The superego is both a figure for the supreme narcissist, and is itself a supreme narcissist. Like the referee in football, the superego is always right, even when he is wrong.

The Freudian superego is a boring and vicious soliloquist with an audience of one. Because the superego, in Freud's view, is a made-up voice – a made-up part – it has a history. Freud sets himself the task of tracing this history with a view to modifying it. And in order to do this he has to create a genealogy that begins with the more traditional, non-secular idea of conscience. Separating out conscience from his new, apparently secular, concept of the superego involves Freud in all the contradictions attendant on unravelling one's history. To put it as simply as possible, Freud's parents, Freud's forebears, like most of the people living in *fin de siècle* Vienna, probably thought of themselves as having consciences; and whatever else they felt about these consciences they were the more or less acknowledged legacy of a religious past, a cultural inheritance. Their consciences were one of the signs of the traditions they belonged to; their more or less shared assumptions about what to do when. Freud wanted to describe what was, in effect, the secular heir of these religious and secularized-religious consciences as the superego. In the telling image in *Civilization and Its Discontents*, Freud writes of the individual as a 'conquered city', living under the regime of the superego.

'We see how one part of the ego,' Freud wrote in *Mourning and Melancholia* (1917), 'sets itself over against the other, judges it critically and, as it were, takes it as its object.' The mind, so to speak, splits itself in two, and one part sets itself over the other to judge it. It 'takes it as its object'; that is to say, the superego treats the ego as though it were an object not a person. In other words, the superego, the inner judge, radically misrecognizes the ego; it treats it, for example, as though it can't answer back, as though it doesn't have a mind of its own (it is noticeable how merciless and unsympathetic we are to ourselves in our self-criticism). It is intimated that the ego – ourselves as we know ourselves to be – is the slave of the superego. How have we become enslaved (to this part of ourselves); or rather, how and why have we consented? What's in it for us, or indeed for someone else? And in what sense is the superego Freud's implied critique of the Judeo-Christian religions and their God?

Internally, there is a judge and a criminal, but no jury.

Annabel Patterson writes in *Early Modern Liberalism* of Algernon Sidney, that 'his agenda was to move the reader gradually to understand that the only guarantor against partisan jurisprudence was shared jurisprudence'. Freud's agenda in psychoanalysis, continuing in this liberal tradition, was the attempt to create – to experiment with the possibility of – shared internal jurisprudence. Self-criticism might be less jaded and jading, more imaginative and less spiteful. The enslaved and judged ego could have more than his judge to appeal to (the psychoanalyst would be the patient's ally in this project, suggesting juries, revealing unconsidered aspects, offering multiple perspectives on underinterpreted actions: underinterpreted, that is, by the patient himself). This, of course, was not possible, at least not in quite this way, in a monotheistic religion, or an absolutist state. To whom could the modern individual appeal in the privacy of his own mind? To which Freud would answer, through the experiment of psychoanalysis, 'there's more to a person – more parts, more voices, more fragmentary alternative selves – than the judge and the judged' (or as Mill, whom Freud translated in his youth, would put it in *On Liberty*, 'the interests of truth require a diversity of opinions'). There is, in effect, a repressed repertoire. Where judgement is, there conversation should be. And we can add, where there is absolute authority, there is the sabotaging of a conversation. Where there is dogma there is an uncompleted experiment. When there is self-condemnation it is always more complicated than that. Mercilessness is cowardice.

The superego, Jean Laplanche and Jean-Bertrand Pontalis write in *The Language of Psychoanalysis*, is 'One of the agencies of the personality as described by Freud . . . the superego's role in relation to the ego may be compared to that of a judge or a censor. Freud saw conscience, self-observation and the formation of ideals as functions of the superego.' It is useful to call the superego an agency, because it has agency; and the complementary alternatives – it is like a censor or a judge – speaks of the punitive, the forbidding and the restrictive. So, paradoxically, being forbidden something – being forbidden to speak, or to act, or to think, or to desire in certain ways – can be itself an unforbidden pleasure. As can turning oneself into an object; the object of censorship and judgement. But what is also perplexing, and adds insult to injury, is that Freud's superego, because it is more than conscience, because it includes this traditional form, is also, in a very limited sense, benign. It is the provider and the guardian of what Freud called our 'ego-ideals'. The ego-ideal, Laplanche and Pontalis write, 'constitutes a model to which the subject attempts to conform'. And, once again, Freud preferred the multiple view: 'Each individual,' he wrote, 'is a component part of numerous groups, he is bound by ties of identification in many directions, and he has built up his ego-ideal on the most various models.' The ego-ideal is both composite – made up from many cultural models and influences – and divisive. It keeps alternative models at bay, but it can also be surprisingly inclusive. In this ambiguity, which Freud could never quite resolve, he was wondering just how constricted the modern individual really is, or has to be. In making the ego-ideal, at its best, the ego has overinterpreted his culture, beginning with the family; he has taken whatever he can use from his culture to make up his own ideals for himself. Whereas the superego as censor or judge, Freud believed, is simply an internalized version of the prohibiting father who says to the Oedipal child: 'Do as I say, not as I do.' But the superego, by definition, despite Freud's telling qualifications, underinterprets the individual's experience (in the Freudian story the father is never imaginative enough about the son, and so vice versa). It is, in this sense, moralistic rather than moral. Like a malign parent, it harms in the guise of protecting; it exploits in the guise of providing good guidance. In the name of health and safety it creates a life of terror and self-estrangement. There is a difference, which makes all the difference, between not doing something out of fear of punishment, and not doing something because one believes it is wrong. Guilt, that is to say, is not necessarily a good clue to what one values; it is only a good clue to what (or whom) one fears. Not doing something because one will feel guilty if one does it is not necessarily a good reason not to do it. Morality born of intimidation is immoral. Psychoanalysis was Freud's attempt to say something new about the police and the judiciary, about the internal legal system.

We can see the ways in which Freud was getting the superego to do too much work for him: it is a censor, a judge, a dominating and frustrating father, and it also carries a blueprint of the kind of person the child should be, and therefore should want to be. It forbids, but it also promotes certain ideals and values. And this reveals the difficulty of what Freud was trying to come to terms with; the difficulty of going on with the cultural conversation about how we describe so-called inner authority, or individual morality. But in each of these multiple functions the ego seems paltry, merely the slave, the doll, the ventriloquist's dummy, the object of the superego's prescriptions: the superego's thing. And the id, the biological drives that drive the individual, are also supposed to be, as far as possible, the victims, the objects of the superego's censorship and judgement. The sheer scale of the forbidden in this system is obscene. And yet, in this vision of things, all this punitive forbidding becomes, paradoxically, one of our primary unforbidden pleasures. We are, by definition, forbidden to find all this forbidding forbidden. Indeed, we find ways of getting pleasure from our restrictedness.

How, in Freud's view, has our virulent, predatory self-criticism become one of our greatest pleasures? How has it come about that we so much enjoy this picture of ourselves as objects, and as objects of judgement and censorship? What is this appetite for confinement, for diminishment, for unrelenting, unforgiving self-criticism? Freud's answer is beguilingly simple: we fear loss of love. Fear of loss of love means forbidding certain forms of love (incestuous love, or interracial love, or same-sex love, or so-called perverse sexuality, and so on). We need, in the first instance, the protection and cooperation of our parents in order to survive; so a deal is made (or, in a different language, there is a social contract). The child says to the parents, 'I will be what you need me to be, as far as is possible, in exchange for your love and protection.' Not unlike Thomas Hobbes's story about sovereignty – in which the sovereign literally makes life liveable – the protection required for survival is paramount: everything must be sacrificed for this, except one's life. Safety is preferred to desire; desire is sacrificed for security. But this supposed safety, at least in Freud's version, comes at considerable cost; at the cost, in effect, of being turned into, by being treated as, an object. It depends upon our being made to feel that we are the kind of creatures that need an excessive amount of critical and condemnatory scrutiny. We must be packed with forbidden desires, if so much censorship and judgement is required. We are being encouraged to believe, by all this censorship and judgement, that forbidden, transgressive pleasures are what we really crave. That really, essentially, deep down, we are criminals; we need to be protected primarily from ourselves, from our wayward desires.

What this regime doesn't allow us to think, clearly, is that we are also packed with, and inspired by, unforbidden desires; or that our moral ideals could be anything other than forbidding (we cannot easily imagine 'the moral ideal being presented as *attractive* rather than *imperative*', as the nineteenth-century philosopher Henry Sidgwick put it in his *The Methods of Ethics*). Just as the overprotected child believes that the world must be very dangerous and he must be very weak if he requires so much protection (and the parents must be very strong if they are able to protect him from all this), similarly we have been terrorized by all this censorship and judgement into believing that we are essentially radically antisocial and, indeed, dangerous to ourselves and others. We must be the only animal that lives as though this grandiose absurdity were true.

IV

The books we read in adolescence often have an extraordinary effect on our lives. They are, among other things, an attempt at regime change. In Freud's language we could say that we free ourselves of our parents' ideals for us by beginning to use the available culture to make up our own ego-ideals, to evolve a sense of our own affinities beyond the family, to speak a language that is more our own. In the self-fashioning of adolescence, reading, for those people who like it – and for many people music and films are much more important – begins to really take, having a subtle and often indiscernible effect throughout a person's life. We should, therefore, note, by way of conclusion, Freud's adolescent passion for *Don Quixote*, a story about a 'madman', as he is frequently referred to in the book, whose life is eventually entirely formed by his reading, in his case by the reading of chivalric romances. Don Quixote is a man who all too literally inhabits, living in and through, the fictions about knights errant that he has consumed. He is a fictional character who makes himself out of fictional characters.

As a young man Freud was an avid reader, and was very good at, and interested in, languages. And he learned

Spanish, as he wrote to a correspondent in 1923, for a particular reason: 'When I was a young student the desire to read the immortal *Don Quixote* in the original of Cervantes led me to learn, untaught, the lovely Castilian tongue.' This 'youthful enthusiasm' was born of a passionate relationship with a school friend called Silberstein. He was, Ernest Jones writes in his biography of Freud,

> Freud's bosom friend in schooldays and they spent together every hour they were not in school. They learned Spanish together and developed their own mythology and private words, mostly derived from Cervantes . . . They constituted a learned society to which they gave the name of Academia Cartellane, and in connection with it wrote an immense quantity of belles-lettres composed in a humorous vein.

An intimacy between two boys that is based on a story about an intimacy between two men (in the service of a woman), an intimacy that inspires writing and humour and complicity. *Don Quixote* could be linked in many ways with Freud's life and the development of psychoanalysis (think of the deluded fantasist and the practical realist, the acquisition of social prestige and the psychopathology of everyday life, the power of language and fiction in the formation of the self, psychoanalytic groups as cults that believe they are not cults – all pertinent to Freud and his work). Learning Spanish and reading *Don Quixote* together with a friend were part of Freud's unofficial education, which ran alongside his official, institutional education (Freud, like Don Quixote himself, was always interested in the unofficial life). But there is one motif that I especially want to single out in this text, so important for Freud and, not incidentally, written more or less contemporaneously with *Hamlet*, for the purposes of thinking further about unforbidden pleasure, and the often futile unforbidden pleasure of self-criticism. And it is, appropriately enough, about Don Quixote's infamous horse, Rocinante.

In a well-known passage in the *New Introductory Lectures* (1933), where Freud described the relationship between the ego and the id – between the person's conscious sense of themselves and their more unconscious desires – he used an all too familiar, all too traditional, analogy (as if to say: psychoanalysis is just a modern version of a very old story, which of course it also is). 'The horse,' Freud wrote,

> supplies the locomotive energy, while the rider has the privilege of deciding on the goal, and of guiding the

powerful animal's movement. But only too often there arises between the ego and the id the not precisely ideal situation of the rider being obliged to guide the horse along the path by which it itself wants to go.

I take this 'not precisely ideal situation' to be an allusion, whatever else it may be in our overinterpreting it, to Don Quixote; and to what, in several senses, he was led by. If we read it in this way, the ego is the deluded fantastical knight who, of course, like all realists, is utterly convinced of (and by) his own plausibility to himself. And Rocinante, in this rather more Beckettian version, is what we call, perhaps appropriately, an old nag. The analogy is at once a parody of, and an exposé of, the cliché of the horse as elemental force. And where does Rocinante go, as Don Quixote is led by his horse? He goes home. But because he is a horse, not a person, home does not mean incest (nor, in all probability, does it mean where his parents are; it just means where he lives). Home, of course, has always meant more than incestuous desire; until, that is, it was under-interpreted by psychoanalysis. In this pre-Freudian and post-Freudian model of the so-called mind – one, perhaps, that Freud repressed in his urge to provide and make compatible a more scientifically bracing and traditionally religious model – the id is the nag Rocinante, the ego is the mad Don Quixote, and the superego is the sometimes amusing, often good-humoured, frequently down to earth and gullible Sancho Panza. 'Sancho,' the critic A. J. Close writes in *Cervantes: Don Quixote*, 'is proverbially rustic; *panza* means 'belly'; and the character of the man is basically that of the clown of sixteenth-century [Spanish] comedy: lazy, greedy, cheeky, loquacious, cowardly, ignorant, and above all, nitwitted.' What does the Freudian superego look like if you take away its endemic cruelty, its unrelenting sadism? It looks like Sancho Panza. And like Sancho Panza, the absurd and obscene superego is a character we must not take too seriously.

'Sancho proves to have too much mother wit to be considered a perfect fool,' Vladimir Nabokov wrote in *Lectures on Don Quixote*, 'although he may be the perfect bore.' We certainly need to think of our superego as a perfect bore, and as all too gullible in its apparent plausibility. We need, in other words, to realize that we may be looking at ourselves a little more from Sancho Panza's point of view, whether or not we are rather more like Don Quixote than we would wish. We might, that is to say, get as much real enjoyment from life, if not more, from our unforbidden pleasures. And we may have underestimated just how restricted our restrictiveness makes us. Our pleasure in each other's company need not be quite so forbidding.

Unforbidden Pleasures

The word *experimental* is apt, providing it is understood
not as descriptive of an act to be later judged in terms of
success and failure, but simply as an act the outcome of
which is unknown.

John Cage, *Silence*

I

We may live in the aftermath of the myth of the Fall, and
the even longer aftermath of the myth of Oedipus, but the
first traffic lights were invented in the United States after the
First World War. The traditional mutual accommodation
travellers had been making to each other on their bikes and
cars and carts was replaced by a set of lights. 'Its purpose,'
the anthropologist James C. Scott writes, 'was to prevent
accidents by imposing an engineered scheme of

coordination.' Partly through pressure of numbers and the proliferation of vehicles, and partly through the new scientific and bureaucratic fantasies of efficiency and productivity, familiar forms of cooperation gave way to a new, technologically implemented, set of rules. People's practical judgement was delegated to a red light. They had known when to stop, but now they were being told when to stop.

Then in 2003, in Drachten in the Netherlands, Hans Monderman, a 'counterintuitive traffic engineer', proposed the removal of traffic lights in the interests of what he called 'shared space'. Once put to the test the results were extraordinary, leading to a series of what were called 'red light removal schemes' across Europe and America. 'He began,' Scott continues,

> with the observation that, when an electrical failure incapacitated traffic lights, the result was improved flow rather than congestion. As an experiment, he replaced the busiest traffic-light intersection in Drachten, handling 22,000 cars a day, with a traffic circle, an extended cycle path, and a pedestrian area. In the two years following the removal of the traffic light, the number of accidents plummeted to only two, compared with thirty-six crashes in the four years prior. Traffic moves more briskly through the intersection when all drivers

know they must be alert and use their common sense, while backups and the road rage associated with them have virtually disappeared. Monderman likened it to skaters in a crowded ice rink who manage successfully to tailor their movements to those of the other skaters. He also believed that an excess of signage led drivers to take their eyes off the road, and actually contributed to making junctions less safe.

It is, of course, in many ways a suggestive experiment; and it is not incidental that Scott uses it in a book entitled *Two Cheers for Anarchism*, anarchism being one of many traditions of antinomian thought, at least in the West. People questioning the rules – wondering both what a rule is, and what it is to follow a rule; wondering what morality really is, and why moral obligations matter – is the news that stays news. We are always tempted to ask, as Sterne does in *The Life and Opinions of Tristram Shandy*: 'is a man to follow rules – or rules to follow him?' Indeed, we are encouraged (that is, educated) to ask in whose interests the rules are made, and for what purpose; whether we are being punished or coerced in the name of being protected. And whether the rules apply to some people but not to others. It has become second nature now for many people to think that rules – even in their most extreme versions,

or particularly in their most extreme versions, as taboos –
may always be no more and no less than human artefacts.
Gravity may be more fundamental than justice, but our
morality doesn't need to have the gravity of gravity. We
are inevitably exercised about where we draw the line,
the kind of lines we draw, and to whom we delegate the
drawing of lines. In certain circumstances killing people
is not forbidden, but killing certain people is; torture is not
forbidden, but torturing certain people, and sometimes
how we torture them, is; sex is not forbidden, but certain
kinds of sexual activity with certain people is; and so on.
Virtually no one sanctions and supports incest or paedophilia. But in every other case, when it comes to the
forbidden – what we mustn't do as opposed to what we
shouldn't do – there are always exceptions, mitigating
circumstances; good reasons found and given for redescribing forbidden acts as newly acceptable, or for having
to do forbidden things (from banning sexism and racism,
say, to suspending civil liberties, to killing 'civilian' children). Apart from the incest taboo, and its displacement in
paedophilia, all the rules seem to be made to be breakable.
This is the familiar legacy of the Enlightenment; this is
what a certain kind of modern person believes. Everything forbidden can be redescribed as ultimately desirable.
Everything sacred can be rendered secular.

But attending to the rules can mean inattention else-
where. Rules are supposed to both attract and organize
our attention, and to be taken for granted. As playing any
game makes clear, the rules have to be wholly absorbing,
and automatically abided by; a second nature to deal with
the first. Rules – and particularly absolute rules, the
guardians of the forbidden – are not supposed to be for-
gettable. Indeed, when it comes to the forbidden we are
not supposed to let our minds wander; we are supposed to
be utterly gripped, and in the grip of the law. The forbidden is by definition defined, is always already defined, so
one cannot be ignorant of it, or casual about it; whether
one is conscious or unconscious of the definition, it is in
principle knowable (knowing what is forbidden may be
one of the main things that knowing is for). Acculturation,
adaptation, means living as if one knows what is forbidden. Psychoanalysis – the theory and therapy that
organizes itself around forbidden desire – adds that we can
be both conscious and unconscious of what is forbidden;
and that being able to redescribe forbidden pleasures as
unforbidden pleasures is the only way to find out what it is
possible to say about them, and what we might want to
argue about. And psychoanalysis, as the only secular therapy that puts the otherwise sacred idea of the forbidden at
the heart of its theory and practice, has also added an

emblematic profession to the culture: one that makes us go on thinking about the forbidden in a secular language; and, by the same token, exposes, as we shall see, not merely what forbidden desire inhibits, but what the whole idea of the forbidden forbids us from considering. The thing, the real thing, that the forbidden has stopped us thinking about is the unforbidden; unforbidden pleasures have suffered at the hands of the more privileged forbidden pleasures. And by being placed in the shade, or rather, by our placing them in the shade, we have forbidden ourselves more pleasure, and more about pleasure, than we may realize.

II

When what is forbidden becomes blurred, or vague, or ambiguous – or is even contested – something is being done to the forbidden. It is being redescribed. The forbidden, by definition, should not be subject to redescription. And yet we know that this is what keeps happening to forbidden pleasures: they keep being reconsidered. We are more and less ambivalent about the forbidden than we want to be. 'A Fundamentall Law in every Common-wealth,' Hobbes wrote in 1651 in *Leviathan* (a book Freud quoted in 1900 in *The Interpretation of Dreams*), 'is that, which being taken away, the Common-wealth faileth, and is utterly dissolved; as a building whose Foundation is destroyed . . . a Fundamentall Law is that, by which Subjects are bound . . .' It was clear to Hobbes that the only foundations that we have are our fundamental laws; that we are the kind of creatures that, without these so-called fundamental laws, will be in a war of all against all; in endless uncivil civil wars. And this presumably is the logic of the forbidden, of the fundamental laws: it is deemed to be that without which we cannot live, or cannot live the lives we most want (or have been persuaded to want). And that we are bewitched by the picture, by the analogy, of having foundations; of there being something upon which everything depends. The two things – the fundamental laws and the foundations – going together. *Leviathan* is a book about what we might be wanting, what we might be thinking and feeling – about, that is, what we might be doing – if we were not paying full attention to these fundamental laws.

In Monderman's traffic experiment – which is not about revising a fundamental law, but is nevertheless suggestive – there are fewer accidents because people are more attentive to what they are doing, more alert, as if the rules make people less sentient; as if something is handed over to the rules, and implicitly to the rule-makers, making people behave automatically, or as sleepwalkers, or as people less inventively competent than they in fact are ('an excess of signage led drivers to take their eyes off the road, and actually contributed to making junctions less safe'). There is more flow than congestion – 'traffic moves more briskly' – but this cuts both ways; it is both more 'efficient', and it increases mobility. Once movement is no longer forbidden by a red light, the unforbidden pleasures of cooperation and its attendant talents reveal themselves. And it is perhaps worth remembering Deleuze and Guattari's use of a similar analogy in their anti-psychoanalytic book *Anti-Oedipus*: 'The prime function incumbent upon the socius [society] has always been to codify the flows of desire, to inscribe them, to record them, to see to it that no flow exists that is not properly dammed up, channeled, regulated.' The forbidden is pictured here as a controlled flow. Whatever it is that flows threatens to get anywhere and everywhere. Hobbes's fundamental laws are to keep an imagined chaos at bay. It is worth bearing in mind, in other words, that the way we imagine desire – the pictures we have, the analogies we use, the figures we find – is often dictated by a forbidding voice. The forbidden defines desire in the same way, it is worth repeating, that the overprotected child believes that there must be something really terrifying out there if he needs so much protection from it.

If Monderman's experiment and Scott's parable are about 'red light removal schemes', they are also about the more or less impeded, regulated, formulated flow of something or other; the question being, what kind of flow does the red light think it is organizing? What is the catastrophe the red light assumes it is wanting to avert? Something, after all, has to be done to desiring, to pleasure, to make it forbidden; it has to be described in a certain way (forbiddingly, intimidatingly). The forbidders have their reasons. When we do forbidden things we often have to give an account of ourselves to ourselves and to others; when we do unforbidden things nothing, apparently, needs to be said.

But what Monderman's experiment revealed, whether or not it is representative, was that there were fewer accidents, virtually no backups or road rage, more fluency and flow, less congestion. And, most interestingly for my purposes, more cooperation with other people and more attentiveness to them, the two things going together ('Monderman likened it to skaters in a crowded ice rink who manage successfully to tailor their movements to those of the other skaters'). It is a picture, however idealized, of sociability as akin to an unwilled choreography; and the idea of tailoring here is genial. As with the skaters there is an attempt at, a shared project of, minimizing frustration and antagonism, and realistically (it actually happens at the skating rink, not just in someone's mind). And all this, not incidentally, can be linked to the conclusions of early infant observation and the kinds of attunement, for example, witnessed between mothers and their babies when things go well enough (and it can also be linked with the Boston Change Process Study Group's salutary point that what matters is not that things go wrong between the mother and baby – how could they not? – but how they are repaired). One of the things the drivers had been forbidden by the red light was a way of working things out with the other drivers. By returning the drivers to an earlier way of doing things, something new was discovered (as Kristin Ross writes in *Communal Luxury*, 'Being attentive to the energies of the outmoded was one way to think oneself into the future'). These drivers and skaters and tailors and anti-Oedipuses and mothers and babies are having to make it up as they go along; not, of course, from scratch, but in the actuality of their immediate circumstance together. However rule-bound their behaviour – and however pastoral a view that may be being promoted by this example – each of these figures is having to acknowledge that, whatever else they are doing, they are experimenting. And the forbidden is clearly where the experimenting is supposed to stop.

III

'The attribution of value to mere conforming behaviour, in abstraction from both motive and consequences, belongs not to morality but to taboo,' the Professor of Jurisprudence H. L. A. Hart wrote in *Law, Liberty, and Morality*, making it clear that to be law-abiding can be to be unaware that one is following a rule. Conformity can be understood only in its particular context. Just as magicians are the people who really know that there is no such thing as magic, conformists can be the people who are not following the rules but living by the magic of rules. Morality can be argued about and consented to, whereas taboos can only be binding, or even spellbinding. Morality, then, is about experimenting with morality; about engaging with it as an ongoing conversation rather than as a rule book: morality as a way of working out, of describing, what we really enjoy doing together.

When it comes to the forbidden we have to distinguish between the authoritarians and the experimentalists, between the essentialists and the pragmatists. The pragmatists, the experimentalists, say, 'I (or someone else) have tried this – have done this forbidden thing – and it had, by our standards, catastrophic consequences. We mustn't let anyone we care about do it again.' The authoritarians, the essentialists, say, 'This is evil, it certainly mustn't be tried, and preferably shouldn't be thought about or discussed. It is what our worst punishments are designed to abolish.' The French psychoanalyst Bela Grunberger was an experimentalist when he wrote that the reason the father should prohibit his son from sleeping with his mother was that, if the son did sleep with his mother he would be unable to satisfy himself or her, and so would be humiliated. In this version of the Oedipus complex the father is not a castrator, but the guardian of the child's future potency. God was being an essentialist in the Old Testament when he told the Jews that 'Thou shalt have no other gods before me'; that they shouldn't worship idols, 'For I the Lord your God am a jealous God, visiting the iniquity of the fathers upon the children unto the third and the fourth generation' (Exodus, 20:3–5). Either way, the forbidden is the foreclosure of certain ways of thinking about the future. The forbidden refers to a future that mustn't happen. Once we know what is forbidden it clears the way for the unforbidden – all those other things that the authorities encourage us to enjoy, or want to fob us off with.

The rules free us to experiment, but an absolute rule – a rule deemed to be beyond conversation, beyond negotiation, as the forbidden is – pre-empts the possibility of improvisation. It is defining. Yet we can never quite know what the forbidden is forbidding us, as Adam and Eve, our first parents, discovered. Once we break the fundamental laws we are in uncharted territory. To forbid something, that is to say, is an omniscient act; it attempts to establish a known future, a future in which certain acts will not be performed, and from which certain thoughts and feelings will be excluded. And that fact has daunting moral implications. Those who lay down and enforce the fundamental laws claim to know what they are, and to know what the consequences are of breaking them. In this sense fundamental laws are prophetic; their makers claim to know the future. And yet, we are all too aware – and psychoanalysis has alerted us to this in a new way – of people's capacity to render the unforbidden forbidden: either to render it, hopefully, inaccessible, and/or to make the unforbidden more exciting. Psychoanalysis has shown us the defensive potential in upping the rhetorical stakes: we can all too easily say to ourselves, 'This is not dangerous, or exciting, or intriguing, this is FORBIDDEN!' (when the Kleinian psychoanalyst Money-Kyrle wrote, as mentioned earlier, that the aim of analysis was to prove the irrelevance of the inhibition, he was alluding to this). In psychoanalysis the analyst works out how it has been worked out by the patient that these are the pleasures he is able and willing to seek, but not those; she works out where the patient wants to draw the line, and why.

When the traffic lights were removed – and this is one of at least two familiar kinds of modern story – the assumed catastrophe did not occur. In fact, as luck, or something else, would have it, things were even better than before. There were fewer accidents, the flow improved, there was less rage, more common sense. Monderman's traffic experiment, as it turned out, was an example of what John Dewey calls, in *Art as Experience*, 'adaptations through expansion (instead of by contraction and passive accommodation)'. The other familiar modern story is that the red lights are removed and futures are created that are beyond our worst imaginings; this is what tragedies and all political tyrannies are there to tell us about. But after Monderman's experiment, Scott writes, 'Small towns in the Netherlands put up one sign boasting that they were "Free of Traffic Signs", and a conference discussing the new philosophy proclaimed "Unsafe is safe".'

We know something of what it is like to drop the idea that there is such a thing as forbidden knowledge; and we do, but mostly don't really, know what it would be like to ban the incest taboo (imagine a society in which children in families, backed up by their parents, were encouraged to murder their mothers and marry their fathers, or murder their fathers and marry their mothers). And we know what it is like for certain forbidden desires to become unforbidden; indeed, some of our most terrible histories, of racism and sexism, are about the forbidding of desires that clearly need not have been forbidden – supposedly forbidden desires – histories that in retrospect seem to some of us to be the fundamental histories of our times; both wildly unintelligible in their cruelty, and all too intelligible. Also the best bits of psychoanalysis have been able to tell us something useful about the anxieties that prompt the forbidding of desires, and about why, therefore, we should not always be overly confident as forbidders of desire (if psychoanalysis had had nothing new to say about restricted acts, or about new ways of completing actions, it would have been of limited value). Once, for example, homophobia is more intelligible – once, that is to say, there are better, more persuasive, stories about it – it becomes contestable.

Nobody now believes that we could, or would even want to, abolish all forbidden desires, any more than anyone could imagine a culture without the category of the unacceptable – the forbidden being the unacceptable at its most intractable ('To unlock the innermost secret of morality and culture is to know, simply: what to avoid,' Philip Rieff wrote in his book *Charisma*). And some of us may believe – and psychoanalysis clearly has a stake in this – that forbidden desires, like everything else, can be redescribed in a way that makes them less forbidden, or certainly less unthinkable. People traditionally come to psychoanalysis because of the monstrousness of their desire, or what they take to be the monstrousness of their desire; and the analyst redescribes where she can. But, obviously, there can be no psychoanalysis – just as, presumably, there can be no culture – without the idea of forbidden desire (even if the history of the making and breaking of rules would suggest – and psychoanalysis has a good story about this – not that rules are made to be broken, but that rules are made to be tested, or can only be made by being tested). No rule is safe, but rules are there supposedly to make us feel safe.

In psychoanalysis we should remember, at least in its developmental stories, that the forbidden is not apparently what we begin with, or where we begin. Babies do not commit forbidden acts, nor do they have, from their own point of view, as it were, forbidden desires. They acquire them – they learn them – through acculturation because their parents, by the time they become parents, have been thoroughly initiated into the forbidden. Little does the very young child know what will be said about what he wants. So what some psychoanalysts refer to as the pre-Oedipal may be, among many other things, a wish to imagine, to picture, a time in the individual's life of intense pleasures and sufferings, that is not lived under the aegis of the forbidden; a time of the intensest feelings before good and evil. The child is born, unavoidably, into a world already governed by the notion of the forbidden; it is the medium in which he grows; and so what is supposedly pre-Oedipal for the baby is in a sense not pre-Oedipal at all, because his parents are thoroughly versed in the whole notion of forbidden desire, and they hold and handle their child accordingly. In this story there is no life before the forbidden, only a life lived before its full realization.

Growing up means growing up into what we call knowledge, or appropriate acknowledgement, of the forbidden. The forbidden is what adults need to tell children about, explicitly and implicitly, consciously and unwittingly. And the forbidden is essentially a story about the consequences of certain kinds of desiring; a catastrophic story, a punitive story, a by definition intimidating story about what can happen if certain desires begin to flow. And we have to wonder what it is like – what the effects are – of children and adolescents growing up in an adult world that is obsessed by forbidden desires and pleasures, often at the cost of the unforbidden ones. And why, by the same token, it might be assumed that promoting unforbidden pleasures could seem to be merely a forlorn consolation for the middle-aged. Forbidden pleasures may have literally stolen the show, and the more intriguing and unpredictable continuity of our lives may lie in our largely unarticulated experiences of unforbidden pleasures, in all their extraordinary variety. The aim of development may be to become as dependent as possible, not as transgressive as possible.

The forbidden and the tragic are made for each other. If tragedy shows us that forbidden desire is really forbidden, comedy (and psychoanalysis) can show us what happens when the unforbidden is forbidden. And what happens when we let the forbidden narrow our minds. The idea of pleasures that are not somehow painful – that are not cures or compensations or alibis for pain – has become literally inconceivable, so wedded are we to our perpetual dismay.

IV

Forbidden desire has been a big problem in the history of the ways we think about ourselves. And I want to explore this in terms of the problem forbidden desire has been for psychoanalysis where it reflects the kinds of problem it has been in the wider culture (and indeed in the culture of *fin de siècle* Vienna, where psychoanalysis began). There is, of course, always a question of what we take desires to be, and of what we can do with and about them; of which ones we are supposed to prefer and why (and why we are supposed to prefer certain desires to others always prompts the question 'Who says?'). A question, in short, of what we have been told, one way and another, about what desiring is, and how we should do it (and this means what we have been told, one way and another by, say, parents, teachers, biologists and novelists, or whoever else we find to be worth listening to, or have had to listen to). But there is a particular sense in which I think that forbidden desire has been a big problem for psychoanalysis; apart, that is, from all the other ways in which it is *the* big problem for psychoanalysis (and not only for psychoanalysis). And it is linked to Monderman's experiment with the traffic as a kind of moral parable.

In his essay 'Gay Betrayals' (From *Is the Rectum a Grave?*), Leo Bersani suggests that gay men, out of what he calls their 'exemplary confusion', should be, or actually are, offering an 'implicit and involuntary message' to heterosexuals that 'we aren't sure of how we want to be social, and that we therefore invite straights to redefine with us the notions of community and sociality'. The forbidden is that which sets absolute limits to redefining notions of community and sociality; and in ways that the unforbidden may not. Is it absurd to imagine a new kind of outlaw, an outlaw in search of unforbidden pleasures? Psychoanalysts, like Bersani's gay men and women, could be the people that take for granted that nobody is sure how she or he wants to be social. The forbidden – the idea of the forbidden, the scenario of forbidden desire – has traditionally been the official way we set limits to how we can want to be social; sociability depending on what we really enjoy doing together, on the pleasures we can take in each other's company.

One might well have thought beforehand that Monderman – akin to Bersani's description of gay men and women being uncertain as to how they want to be social – was taking a considerable risk with his 'red light removal schemes', despite what he ultimately discovered. Forbidding things can stop people both finding new ways and recovering old ways of collaborating. Forbidding things can pre-empt the enjoyment of unforbidden things. What forbidding things is an obstacle to is not always clear. Clearly the sociability created by the red lights is different from the sociability created without them. So what I want to consider is: what have been the consequences of the forbidden dominating the ways we think about pleasure and sexuality (in psychoanalysis)? If we take forbidden pleasure as the essence of pleasure, as the real pleasure, what happens to the unforbidden pleasures? Do they really exist – are they derivatives, substitutes, sublimations? – and if they do what kinds of pleasures are they? Are they all poor relatives of the real thing? Are they merely for the timid, the inhibited, the cowardly, the dull? Is unforbidden pleasure merely hedonism for infants and the elderly? By privileging transgression we may have created a spurious belief of all too knowing pleasure-seekers, who supposedly have all the best lines and all the best lives, however tragic. Perhaps psychoanalysis, in its original overvaluing of forbidden desire, has been complicit with what D. H. Lawrence in his Introduction to *Pansies* called 'the modern mind . . . falling into this form of degraded taboo-insanity'; that is, the insanity generated, in Lawrence's view, by the whole notion of taboo. It may be worth wondering again what unforbidden pleasures, of which there are so many, amount to in the story, and in the experience of, a life.

Clearly, if we believe for example that real pleasure, profound pleasure, passionate pleasure, is forbidden, or derives from the forbidden, then courage is what we need, and risk is what we will celebrate (and idealize). We will need to be as brave as possible in not betraying our desire; indeed, to promote unforbidden pleasures is to imagine a world in which we don't have to take courage (or cowardice) very seriously. There certainly seems to be an old-fashioned story about heroism lurking somewhere in our commitment to the forbidden in which the bold, the risk-taking, the transgressive are, by definition, having a better time (this, of course, might make psychoanalysis, then, a kind of military training, helping people become more the heroes and heroines of their own desires). If one of my greatest pleasures in life is my morning coffee, am I, in some sense, a rather pathetic person, too starkly, as people used to say, bourgeois? If being as kind as is possible gives me the life I want, am I some kind of weakling, merely part of what Nietzsche called a 'slave religion'? If I prefer friendship, or political activism, to sexual relationships or sexual encounters, am I just inhibited? Are the seekers of unforbidden pleasures – who are also, of course, the seekers of forbidden pleasures; they can't help but be that also – too bland (that is, terrified) for real consideration, other than the consideration of analysing them out of it? Are they great sublimators and displacers but poor realists? We don't have to choose in psychoanalysis between the forbidden and the unforbidden, but we sort of do; we can and will have forbidden and unforbidden pleasures but we always already know where the real action is. In short, what, from a psychoanalytic point of view, is the unforbidden? Where do unforbidden pleasures stand in psychoanalytic stories about a good life? Are unforbidden pleasures sad substitutes for the forbidden ones? What has the monism of forbidden pleasure – the siren-song, the

abiding claim on the Freudian subject of the forbidden –
stopped us from thinking about pleasure?

In his book on Isaiah Berlin, the political philosopher
John Gray describes what he calls Berlin's 'agonistic liberalism' as a 'liberalism of conflict among inherently
rivalrous goods'; a liberalism in which it is assumed that,
because there is never only one good that we seek, there
will always be conflict; and where there is no conflict
there has been tyranny. By persuading us that forbidden
and unforbidden pleasures are not inherently rivalrous
goods, that we should be suspicious of our desire for the
unforbidden pleasures, psychoanalysis may have over-
simplified us, given us an impoverished picture of our
pleasure-seeking, and of ourselves as pleasure-seekers.
Psychoanalysis, it seems, has repressed the unforbidden,
refused to elaborate it, wanting to not take it too seriously;
or has simply interpreted it as a refuge from, or a disguised,
watered-down version of, the real, horrifyingly exciting
thing: forbidden desire.

It is possible that privileging forbidden pleasures grossly
narrows the pleasures people can take in each other; over-
determines and confines their moral thinking about what
they want to do to and with each other; and so has prevented psychoanalysis from helping people to develop
new styles of relating, or what Michel Foucault called

'new relational modes'. The forbidden has perhaps been overly forbidding (the very idea of the forbidden may, for example, be a way of making us hate sex, as some kind of unbearable ordeal). And perhaps there is nothing more conservative – in both senses – than a commitment to certain versions of the forbidden (the desire for justice, for example, in its various political forms, is not, it should be noted, intrinsically a forbidden desire). What would our lives be like – and what would the therapy and practice of psychoanalysis be like – if we took forbidden pleasures and unforbidden pleasures as inherently rivalrous goods? That is, if we didn't take it for granted that forbidden pleasure was the real pleasure, or the only real pleasure? If we thought of people seeking a multiplicity of pleasures, without a pre-assumed hierarchy of pleasures? None of this, it should be said, necessitates relegating the erotic. It is, after all, worth remembering, in the psychoanalytic way, that many of the pleasures of childhood are unforbidden.

We can do a number of different things with the category of the forbidden, as we can with any of the familiar binaries that we have learned not to be too impressed by. Forbidding is censorship at its most hyperbolic. And it has forbidden our thinking about the unforbidden ('. . . sun destroys / The interest of what's happening in the shade', Philip Larkin wrote in 'The Whitsun Weddings'). We are familiar, now, with the more celebrated, more researched, more historicized, story about what ideas about sanity have done to and for ideas about madness, or indeed, about the rational and the irrational as having been mutually defining. Or about how heterosexuality has formed and deformed homosexuality, and vice versa. It should be no less integral to psychoanalysis – and not only to psychoanalysis – to track the effects of privileging, if not always preferring, the forbidden pleasures to the unforbidden ones. It can always, after all, be two-way traffic. The parts of ourselves that desire forbidden pleasures might have a lot to learn from the parts of ourselves that desire the unforbidden. The seekers of unforbidden pleasures may know something about pleasure that has never occurred to the transgressive; about the pleasures, for example, of not being single-minded. Or about what the pleasures that don't require courage might be able to tell us about the pleasures that do; about what the pleasures of fellow-feeling, say, or of friendship might have to do with erotic relations, and their inevitable violence. Or about the difference between intimidation and pleasure; or the difference between mastery and skill, and what the alternatives to mastery might be. And we don't always need to think of pleasures as comparable; only when competition becomes more important than exchange in human relations do pleasures seem merely rivalrous. There is the intelligence of knowing what one can bear and enjoy, and the intelligence of knowing what one thinks one should be able to bear and enjoy.

It is my impression, and it is only that, that even though analysts are not supposed to encourage their patients to talk about anything specifically, they encourage their patients to talk rather more about their forbidden pleasures than their unforbidden ones. So the unforbidden pleasures are taken to be a clue about the other kinds. Analysts may tend to listen out for trauma, and for forbidden desire; and, indeed, for the trauma of forbidden desire. But when everybody supposedly knows the only currency is the forbidden, what are we going to be able to hear and to say? If, as Isaiah Berlin wrote in *Four Essays on Liberty*, 'the necessity of choosing between absolute claims is an inescapable characteristic of the human condition', then it is worth wondering what would happen – what psychoanalysis would sound like, and what the wider culture would be like – if it took the pursuit of unforbidden pleasures as one of a person's absolute claims, or as one of the absolute claims everyone has to deal with.

There is that which we are unable or unwilling to talk about because it is forbidden ('censored', to use Freud's word); and there is that which resists or is recalcitrant to articulation – what Seamus Heaney called 'pre-reflective lived experience', and we might call the pre-symbolic or proto-symbolic experience of the younger child. But between these two dramatic and poignant forms of self-protection and inevitable opacity there is something both more accessible and less patent; that which we wouldn't bother to elaborate – it might have seemed too trivial, too bland, too everyday and too ordinary to make anything of: neither forbidden, nor apparently obscure. These unforbidden pleasures may be more or less taken for granted, and by the same token enjoyed as unconsidered trifles, relatively conflict free (unless we assume they are merely sublimated forms of forbidden pleasures). There are the pleasures we mostly don't have, and can't easily talk about; and there are the unforbidden pleasures which we either don't bother to talk much about, or talk about all too fluently; without apparent shame, or guilt, or much embarrassment (pleasures unrelated, say, to economic gain or prestige). Indeed, we all too easily think of the unforbidden pleasures as especially sociable ones (more broadly sociable, more communal). It has been one of the mixed blessings of British psychoanalysis – part of its interest, and for some people part of its resistance to Freud – that it has spoken up for these unforbidden pleasures (of affection, of friendship, of play, of imagination). That it has wanted to make the unforbidden pleasures as interesting, as intriguing, as formative, as the forbidden pleasures. And in Marion Milner's work to have even made the erotic of a piece with the unforbidden.

V

'One of the central puzzles of English history,' the American historian Ethan Shagan writes in *The Rule of Moderation*, is 'how England came to represent reason, civility and moderation to a world it slowly conquered.' Freud, who was himself, interestingly, an Anglophile, didn't want psychoanalysis, as we know, to be thought of as a Jewish science (though, just to adequately complicate things, Ernest Jones notes in his biography that Freud had a 'long-standing admiration for Oliver Cromwell' and that 'Cromwell's reintroduction of the Jews into England must have been a considerable factor in this'). And, of course, when psychoanalysis came to England in the early years of the twentieth century – that is, before Melanie Klein, the Freuds and other European émigrés arrived – it was not a predominantly Jewish profession. And none of the prominent members of what later emerged after the Second World War as the Middle or Independent Group – most notably Winnicott, Rycroft, Milner, Khan, Laing,

Klauber, Lomas – was Jewish. England was, in other words, both congenial and very foreign to Freud's psychoanalysis, as Freud's psychoanalysis was to the English. Psychoanalysis, that is to say, arrived in an England that had come to represent 'reason, civility and moderation' to a world that it had quite recently slowly conquered. It was the England of Darwin and Darwinism – and Freud himself was committed to Darwinian biology – but Darwin himself in his English way was a paragon of reason, civility and moderation while his ideas slowly conquered the world. And England was also a country, as many people have pointed out, with a literary tradition preoccupied by childhood. In retrospect it is not surprising that psychoanalysis would find a home there; and not surprising that psychoanalysis would be changed in the process, most notably through the pioneering of child analysis by Klein, Anna Freud, Winnicott and John Bowlby.

By the end of the Second World War, the British analysts, as they were now referred to, had learned a lot about early development from children evacuated during the war, and from their mothers who had had to go out and do war work while their husbands were away. But the Middle or Independent Group – unlike the warring Kleinians and Freudians in the British Society – would come to represent, for better and for worse, something akin to reason, civility and moderation to the psychoanalytic world. If, in psychoanalysis, only the exaggerations are true, in this version of British psychoanalysis, exaggeration – the metaphysical, the non-empirical, the enthusiastic – was suspect (Winnicott was a paediatrician, Bowlby was interested in ethology). As is well known, none of them took up Freud's idea of the Death Instinct, and all of them took the (observed) so-called mother–infant dyad as seriously, sometimes more seriously, as they took sexuality (in England, at least, they were not going to sacrifice reason, civility and moderation to sexuality). And all of them, implicitly in what was called their developmental object relations theories, were critical of the conquering of the world that was colonization, and more recently fascism; implicitly because none of them was overtly political. But their developmental theories were a critique of imperialism. The psychoanalytic child they described was a born imperialist who needed to become a democrat. They wanted relationships, not exploitative forms of gratification; they wanted the cooperative, not the predatory, in human relations. So they were all radically anti-imperialist in their accounts of mothering and adult sexuality, and, indeed, in their accounts of the role of the analyst; the child's adapting to what cannot be adapted to without distortion and deformation was their theme (slightly less

guarded was Masud Khan's implicit critique of colonialism
in his theory of perversions). Imperialism, colonization, had
become the newly forbidden, the culturally unacceptable
that psychoanalysis would be recruited, in Britain, to explain
and to ameliorate. It would be too crude, but partly true I
think, to say that it was the potential imperialism of sexuality – and the wish to see satisfaction as collaborative and
mutual – that informed these British analysts' theory and
practice; and that could make mothers and babies, paradoxically, their preferred objects of psychoanalytic desire. This
made their writing seem at once Freudian and profoundly
anti-Freudian at the same time; and often somewhat
anti-Kleinian (the Kleinians were the new imperialists, col-
onizing the minds of their patients). But it is possible to see
now that what they were doing was trying to link, or even
to make compatible, Freud's theories about sexuality and
the forbidden – the Oedipal and pre-Oedipal predicament
of the Freudian child – with the unforbidden pleasures of
infancy and childhood. They were trying to join the language of British romanticism to the language of Freudian
psychoanalysis; a language that, as Freud acknowledged,
was originally based on Darwinian biology, but which privileged exchange over competition in human relationships.
Competition is limiting in ways that exchange need not be.

When you put together the profoundly innocent child

of a Protestant British romanticism with the infantile
sexuality of the Freudian child you get the Middle or Independent Group in British psychoanalysis. The child of
Wordsworth and Coleridge and Blake is notably and naturally kind, sympathetic and full of fellow-feeling, and he
has a virtually instinctive capacity and need to forget himself, to absorb himself in things (and people) other than
himself. Given the chance he loses himself in nature, in
books, in games. He or she is by nature both solitary and
sociable and so hates – as the novels of Dickens, Eliot
and D. H. Lawrence make poignantly clear – tyranny,
submission and injustice. The child is not without vigor-
ous, even daemonic, antisocial energies – the energy that
could be for Blake 'eternal delight', and the energy that
Wordsworth knew to be also violently destructive – but
what is pointedly recognized about this romantic child is
his natural kindness and his desire to forget himself, to
lose himself, to become absorbed. And the extraordinary
vitality of his desire; both his keen and amused hedonism,
and his ruthlessness. He has an openness to the world that
growing up endangers, and that endangers him in the contemporary economic and political reality of the late
eighteenth and early nineteenth century. It is the adults
who do the terrible, forbidden things; in growing up natural innocence is replaced by unoriginal sin. But it is the

intensity of these unforbidden pleasures of childhood that
the romantics and the novelists promote; and that is taken
up, wittingly and unwittingly, in the Freudian work of
Winnicott, but more particularly in the work of Marion
Milner. What Winnicott started off with his idea of play –
that, crucially for him, was an essential capacity un-
disrupted by instinctual desire – Milner elaborated in terms
of the child's capacity for absorption, and all that that en-
tailed. In Milner's work – and we should remember that she
was supervised by Melanie Klein and analysed by Winnicott – the forbidden and unforbidden pleasures of childhood
are seen to be interanimating, inextricable, and never mutually exclusive. Indeed for Milner, pathology involved the
splitting of the forbidden and the unforbidden. For Milner,
as a psychoanalyst, there is something before transgression, before the forbidden; something unforbidden that
partly makes the forbidden possible; or is the precondition
for the experience of forbidden desire.

VI

Concluding her 1956 paper 'Psychoanalysis and Art', Milner put her cards on the table. 'The central idea of my
paper,' she wrote,

is that the unconscious mind, by the very fact of its not clinging to the distinction between self and other, seer and seen, can do things that the conscious logical mind cannot do. By being more sensitive to the samenesses rather than the differences between things, by being passionately concerned with finding 'the familiar in the unfamiliar' (which, by the way, Wordsworth says is the whole of the poet's business), it . . . brings back blood to the spirit, passion to intuition. It provides the source for all renewal and rebirth, when old symbols have gone stale. It is, in fact, what Blake calls 'each man's poetic genius'.

We might baulk now at the anachronism of some of the language, or perhaps of the central idea; even though, in Freud's mythology, it is the work of Eros that Milner was describing. But I want to use Milner's conclusion here as an emblem of what I am talking about. From this account we could say: the forbidden is the apotheosis, the final formulation of the supposedly not-me, of the wished-for not-me. It draws an uncrossable line; it separates me from what I want, but should not want. But the unconscious mind, in Milner's almost old-fashioned picture, is 'more sensitive to the samenesses rather than the differences'; is not 'clinging to the distinction between self and other'; has a passion for finding, in Wordsworth's words – and it is not incidental that Blake and Wordsworth are invoked here – 'the familiar in the unfamiliar' (and that could mean, in this context, finding the unforbidden in the forbidden; or acknowledging that forbidden pleasures can be distortions or perversions of unforbidden pleasures). Milner's version of the unconscious mind is not, it should be noted, primarily seeking forbidden (incestuous) pleasure, it is seeking unforbidden reunions; the pleasures of sameness, not the pleasures of transgression (where there is no difference there can be no transgression). This is Milner's theme. The recovery of oneself as a part of one's world, rather than an exile from it (the forbidden exiles us from ourselves, for better and for worse). These are the formative experiences for her; not the horrifying, exciting urgencies of incestuous desire, but what she named, quoting the art historian Bernard Berenson, 'the aesthetic moment'.

It is what she called the 'central idea' that emerged in her great paper of 1952, 'The Role of Illusion in Symbol Formation':

The basic identifications which make it possible to find new objects, to find the familiar in the unfamiliar, require an ability to tolerate a temporary loss of sense of self, a temporary giving up of the discriminating ego which stands apart and tries to see things objectively and rationally without emotional colouring. It perhaps requires a state of mind which has been described by Berenson as 'the aesthetic moment'. 'In visual art, the aesthetic moment is that fleeting instant, so brief as to be almost timeless, when the spectator is at one with the work of art he is looking at . . .'

It is the aesthetic moment in visual art that Milner wants to use as a model for human relations; the at-oneness in which the distinction between the self and the other, the forbidden and the unforbidden, briefly disappears (and she also makes us wonder, in this context, what abstract art has to be to make it a forbidden pleasure). Milner went on to suggest, in the Winnicottian way, that the patient in analysis, like the child in the family, needs what she calls 'the factor of a capacity in the environment':

It is the capacity of the environment to foster this growth, by providing conditions in which a recurrent partial return to the feeling of being one is possible; and I suggest that the environment does this by the recurrent providing of a framed space and time and a pliable medium, so that, on occasions, it will not be necessary for self-preservation's sake to distinguish clearly between inner and outer, self and not-self.

This 'feeling of being one', this 'giving up of the discriminating ego', need not be forbidden, but it could be. It might be described as transgressive, but it need not be; just as such states could be described as omnipotent or as denial of envy or dependence, or aggression, or indeed of separateness. Clearly cultures – and schools of psychoanalysis – can be distinguished by how much these states of togetherness are encouraged or tolerated (and indeed describe), and in what ways these states are understood. But in these states – which Milner was careful to describe as fleeting, momentary, 'partial' returns to the feeling of being one – a rule is not being broken; rather, an experience is being risked: the experience of what happens when vigilant self-holding is relinquished so that one becomes of a piece with the world. One makes the world one's own by forgetting oneself. Sameness is not merely recuperative for Milner, it is the way we recover the future; it makes it possible to, in her words, 'find new objects'. The acknowledgement of sameness makes the idea of transgression disappear. Finding new objects, in other words, in this story, does not involve a so-called resolution of the Oedipus complex. It involves broaching the unforbidden pleasures, not the forbidden ones. The forbidden keeps us different from ourselves; the unforbidden keeps us the same as ourselves. We may need at least both.

One of the unforbidden pleasures of childhood for Blake and Wordsworth was the child's capacity to be absorbed. It is the loss of that capacity which Milner believed modern people suffer from (and come to analysis for). Of course she knew about people's real trouble with forbidden desire, but this was her more singular contribution to psycho-analysis. In 1934, in *A Life of One's Own*, she wrote of her need for 'a method for discovering one's true likes and dislikes, for finding and setting up a standard of values that is truly one's own and not a borrowed mass-produced ideal'. What Hobbes called a 'Fundamentall Law' – that which is absolutely forbidden – is perhaps the exemplary or ultimate 'borrowed mass-produced ideal' ('the innermost secret of morality and culture is to know, simply: what to avoid'). All essences and foundations are the equivalent of mass-produced ideals; invitations to conformity. The forbidden informs us of what our true likes and dislikes must be. Could it follow from this that the unforbidden does not? Or that, as Milner intimated, we have done it all the wrong way round; we have used the forbidden pleasures to tell us what the unforbidden pleasures are, rather than allowing the unforbidden pleasures to be a way of discovering one's true likes and dislikes. Milner's quest, one could say, was for what Seamus Heaney in *Crediting Poetry* called 'a less binary and altogether less binding vocabulary'.

This book is about whether the unforbidden pleasures have something more to tell us, or at least something else to tell us, about pleasure than the forbidden ones. Were this to be true, a lot of things that we have taken very seriously would seem less serious. The tyranny of the forbidden is not that it forbids, but that it tells us what we want – to do the forbidden thing. The unforbidden gives no orders.

VII

'Philosophers,' Joyce Appleby writes in *The Relentless Revolution: A History of Capitalism*, 'use the word "reify" to indicate when a concept is being talked about as a real thing rather than as a way of talking about something.' The forbidden, we might say, has been reified when it is really a way of talking about something, about many things. But the forbidden has to be presented, above all, as the ultimately real thing, a way of talking about what Hobbes referred to as the fundamental laws; the rules governing what it is forbidden for us to do are the rules upon which all the other rules depend. And we have to appear to know what we are talking about when we talk about the forbidden — we are talking about what we absolutely must not do, and therefore what we must not be. We are supposed to be those people who would not dream of doing forbidden things. So talking about the forbidden is talking about who we really are; or rather, who we wish we were, because somewhere in ourselves we know that things are forbidden not only because people are tempted to do them, but because we live in a world in which people do these things, in which people do have apparently forbidden pleasures (it should be noted that in the history of capitalism the forbidden has been a remarkably flexible concept). To talk about the forbidden is to talk, then, about risk and transgression, about certain kinds of excitement and fear and shame. It leads us towards our so-called darker selves. And it also leads us towards our more militant and authoritarian selves.

But if to talk about the forbidden is essentially to define ourselves, is a way of saying who we would prefer ourselves to be, what is talking about the unforbidden a way of talking about? What kind of people do we sound like when we talk about our unforbidden pleasures? Perhaps not that impressive, or impressive in ways that haven't yet occurred to us. Promoting unforbidden pleasures means finding new kinds of heroes and heroines (or dispensing with them altogether). It certainly privileges the more ordinary at the cost of whatever we take to be the alternatives to the ordinary. So these questions are a way of wondering what pleasures, if any, can really sustain us. Of wondering whether life without significant aspiration is viable for us.

Forbidden desire, in its mostly religious forms, has clearly been very sustaining – as an organizing of desire, as a maintaining of essential meaning and value, as a way of feeling that our lives are worth living because something is really at stake in living our lives as well as possible (that is, as obediently as possible). Though each of these religious forms assumes that the pleasure we can take in each other is insufficient; that something transcendent or supernatural is required to really keep us going. Considering the unforbidden pleasures (alongside the forbidden ones) and whether they can make life sufficiently convincing – pleasurable enough to be going on with, even preferable to their forbidden counterparts – means wanting a new sense of what, if anything, we want to keep us going; of what, if anything, we find our real enjoyment in; and whether that is enough.

Life Itself

It will amount to something
I was told, and I was told to hold fast to decency,
to be spotlit and confident. I was told
next year's words await another voice.

Joanna Klink, 'Elemental'

I

However painful one's life turns out to be – however painful one believes that life really is – it is also possible that we have been forbidden from enjoying our lives, or from enjoying them as much as we might. Indeed, our sense of injustice – including all of our personal and our more obviously political grievances – is based on this simple idea: that we are being refused possible pleasures. This is what the so-called difference between the generations always entails. It is, after all, a common enough accusation of the young that adults are unnecessarily restrictive; that they are always setting limits to the available pleasure (Freud's story about the Oedipus complex is an emblem of this). So it is often of interest – even though it is something, we might say, that is happening all the time – when someone's older self addresses their younger self, in a way that the younger self can never converse with itself. That is, from the point of view of the desires and ideals of the younger self, more or less satisfied, more or less realized. The older self always knows more than (if not about) the younger self only in the sense that the older self knows more about the consequences of the younger self's desiring. Our older selves go on living the what-happened-next of our wanting.

In 'An Attempt at Self-Criticism', a new introduction to the second (1886) edition of *The Birth of Tragedy: Out of the Spirit of Music* of 1872, Nietzsche attempts to explain why – in retrospect, as a middle-aged man – he had written this extraordinary book, at the extraordinarily young age of twenty-eight. At the age of forty-two, reviewing his first book, Nietzsche is quite clear about the question he was trying to answer as a younger man. 'The finest, most beautiful, most envied race of men ever known, the people who made life seem most seductive, the Greeks,' he wrote, '– what, they of all people *needed* tragedy? Or even: art?' What could tragedy possibly have to do with the finest, the most beautiful, the most envied race of men ever known? What could possibly trouble such ideal people, whose very perfection, one would have thought, made their lives virtually flawless? The best people must be those who are – by definition, by a certain kind of logic – exempt from the worst things in life. Why would people so impressed, so intoxicated, by life make tragedy their chosen genre; why, indeed, if life itself was abundantly sufficient, would they need art at all?

Perhaps all art, all culture, Nietzsche suggested, is a kind of protection racket, fobbing us off to keep the horror at bay. The Greeks may have needed art, say, to celebrate this 'over-brimming' wonderful life. But why, we could then ask, would it need to be celebrated at all, rather than just simply lived? What does celebration add, and why would anything need to be added to such consummate lives? But, above all, why did it even occur to these enviable Greeks that there was such a thing as tragedy? Nietzsche's question, addressed to his younger self, is, in other words: what is it that even the achieved perfectibility of man – as represented by the ancient Greeks – can't free us from, or protect us against? Even if we meet, even if we satisfy, our cultural ideals – that is, become the people we most want to be – what will we be left with? This is exactly the kind of question an older person is more likely to ask than a younger one. And why this should be so – why aging as disillusionment has become such an ingrained cliché – is also worth wondering about. Following on from Nietzsche's question we could ask how it has come about that we have been educated to have expectations about life that are so likely to leave us feeling defeated. We must have been wanting the wrong things from life – we must have inherited the wrong cultural ideals – if our experience is one of cumulative disappointment.

Regretting much about his youthful book, Nietzsche particularly deplored having been seduced, as a younger man, by the language and the values of the men he admired and had emulated. 'I now regret very much,' he wrote, 'that I did not yet have the courage (or immodesty?) at that time to permit myself a language of my very own for such personal views and acts of daring, labouring instead to express strange and new evaluations'; meaning here in the language of older philosophers, particularly of Immanuel Kant and Arthur Schopenhauer. One thing, Nietzsche intimated, that might lead one to despair and defeatedness is not speaking in one's own voice; letting admired others speak on one's own behalf; having pleasures that are not our own foisted on us. These admiring loyalties that Nietzsche increasingly believed – partly inspired by his reading of Ralph Waldo Emerson – prevented one doing the one thing most necessary, the most life-justifying thing: becoming who one is. It is as though what had dawned on Nietzsche was the difference between asking yourself, 'Who do I admire?' and asking yourself, 'Who do I want to admire?' But what Nietzsche went on to quote as an example, from Schopenhauer's *The World as Will and Representation* (1818), went to the heart of Nietzsche's dilemma; of the young man who wrote the book, and of the middle-aged man who then reintroduced it to himself and his readers: 'What gives to everything tragic, whatever the form in which it appears, the characteristic tendency to the sublime,' Schopenhauer wrote, 'is the dawning of the knowledge that the world and life can afford us no true satisfaction, and are therefore not worth our attachment. In this the tragic spirit consists; it leads to resignation.' Once we realize what life is really like – 'the world and life can afford us no true satisfaction' – we are doomed, at best, to resignation, something Nietzsche claimed was utterly 'alien' to him. Parodying Kant's famous motto in *What is Enlightenment?* (1784) – 'Dare to know!' – Nietzsche recruited Schopenhauer here to say, in a wholesale rejection of progressive, enlightened, liberal values: 'Dare to know that the world and life can afford us no true satisfaction.' And therefore whatever our values are, they can afford us no true satisfaction. Dare to know that only one thing is worth knowing, which is that it would have been better never to have had to enter into the knowing game. But Schopenhauer, he now felt, had seduced him into a false pessimism. Schopenhauer, Nietzsche claimed, had 'obscured and ruined' his 'Dionysiac intimations'. There are then two kinds of despair for the middle-aged Nietzsche: the despair of being lured into using other people's words for one's own new evaluations; and the despair of being seduced into faux despair. Despair, the Dionysian Nietzsche believes, is always a temptation, especially for those who are frightened of life. They effectively take refuge in imitation, and the joys of defeatedness. 'What, after all, could be more consoling,' Diana Fuss writes in *Dying Modern*, 'than the knowledge that there can be no consolation?'

And yet this quotation from Schopenhauer that the older Nietzsche was so disdainful of – but can't resist quoting and so recirculating – echoes, or reinforces, one of the most dramatic moments in *The Birth of Tragedy*. Wanting to explain what he calls the 'fantastic super-abundance of life' of the Olympian gods, which reflected 'the over-brimming, indeed triumphant existence' of the ancient Greeks, Nietzsche suggested that the modern spectator stands 'in some perplexity' before all this enviable vitality, 'asking himself what magic potion these people can have drunk which makes them see . . . the ideal image of their own existence'. The implication here is that the Greeks have idealized themselves, and indeed life itself; and if they have done this, there must be a reason why idealization was required. And it is this that Nietzsche described the modern spectator as having already 'turned away from'. ' "Do not go away," ' Nietzsche exhorted the reader, the modern spectator:

'but listen first to what popular Greek wisdom has to say about this inexplicably serene existence you see spread out before you here.' An ancient legend recounts how King Midas hunted long in the forest for the wise Silenus, companion of Dionysus, but failed to catch him. When Silenus has finally fallen into his hands, the King asks what is the best and most excellent thing for human beings. Stiff and unmoving, the daemon remains silent until, forced by the King to speak, he finally breaks out in shrill laughter and says: 'Wretched, ephemeral race, children of chance and tribulation, why do you force me to tell you the very thing which it would be most profitable for you *not* to hear? The very best thing is utterly beyond your reach: not to have been born, not to *be*, to be *nothing*. However, the second best thing for you is: to die soon.'

It is somehow appropriate that, in a book called *The Birth of Tragedy*, real birth is discouraged. In one fell swoop all of our cultural ideals are invalidated; as, indeed, is the whole idea of cultural ideals. It is reactive to what Nietzsche called 'the terrible wisdom of Silenus' that the Greeks created their super-abundant, over-brimming vision of life: 'The Greeks knew and felt the terrors and horrors of existence; in order to live at all they had to place in front of these things the resplendent, dream-born figures of the Olympians.' They needed their idealized cosmology. Yet 'all the shimmering light of the Olympian gods paled before the wisdom of Silenus'. This wisdom of Silenus, which overlaps with Schopenhauer's wisdom, this 'true knowledge, this insight into the terrible truth, which outweighs every motive for action', Nietzsche continued, creates 'revulsion'. And for this primal revulsion, this fundamental revelation, there are two self-cures, in his view: the ecstasies of Dionysus or the 'resignation' of Hamlet. Elemental exuberance or fatal lethargy. 'Very powerful forces are required to defeat the forces of desire [and] lead them to resignation,' Deleuze and Guattari write in *Anti-Oedipus*. It is this powerful, overriding force of Silenus's wisdom that Nietzsche feels himself seduced and disarmed by. This was why the serene Greeks were obsessed by tragedy. Because the truth about life is that it would have been better not to have been born. And we have been born, and been given this belated knowledge. A knowledge that makes a mockery of our desire; that reveals all our purposes as hiding places and refuges. At least life has taught us this: that life is unbearable.

Not the Platonic or Socratic redemption by knowledge and virtue, nor the Aristotelian flourishing of excellence and potential, nor the saving laws and graces of the Judeo-Christian religions, were plausible or viable forms of optimism, in Nietzsche's view. Indeed, there were none. 'The very fact,' Raymond Geuss writes in a commentary on *The Birth of Tragedy*,

> that the Athenians organized so much of their political, social, and religious life around a ritualized representation of catastrophic destruction (i.e. tragedy) shows that they must in some sense have been metaphysical pessimists. How else, Nietzsche argues, could one explain the keen, addictive pleasure the Athenians and, following them, many others through the ages have taken in watching a basically admirable, heroic individual destroy himself in the pursuit of truth and knowledge, as Oedipus does?

If the pursuit of our highest cultural ideals – truth and knowledge – destroys us, our highest cultural ideal must be self-destruction. Unless, that is, we have the wrong ideals. But then what should these ideals be? What kind of cultural ideals could we have if 'the world and life can afford us no true satisfaction'? If the 'very best thing is utterly beyond [our] reach' and it is, in fact, 'not to have been born, not to *be*, to be *nothing*'? 'Nietzsche asks,' Peter Berkowitz writes in his book *Nietzsche: The Ethics of an Immoralist*, 'how an infectious optimism, an over-brimming cheerfulness, a manly healthiness, epitomized by the Greeks' savage and sensual myths, could emerge in full awareness of man's inherently miserable lot.' We might say: it could only emerge once that full awareness was fully acknowledged. If there can be no true satisfaction – if there is only (psychic) alchemy, idealization, bravado, self-deception, the art that Nietzsche claims we have that we might not perish of the truth – then the implication is clear. Either we seek, or have been educated to seek, the wrong satisfactions, or we are living in the wrong world, a world utterly unsuited to our nature. Since, at least for secular and modern people, there is no other world, we must, as Nietzsche intimated, have the wrong cultural ideals. It can only be better not to have been born if either what happens subsequently is unbearably painful, or if we have – at least in part – made it unbearably painful through the wildly inappropriate cultural ideals that we have construed for ourselves. This is what Nietzsche's phrase 'the transvaluation of all values' refers to. We have unsuited ourselves for the world as we find it. So we end up thinking of it as a world well lost. Or we end up thinking, as Nietzsche did in *The Birth of Tragedy*, that we must choose Dionysus or Hamlet.

And yet it was reactive to Silenus's apparent wisdom and Schopenhauer's metaphysics that Nietzsche became the philosopher who invented a new kind of modern person, a person who could conceive of himself as undefeated, unembittered, unintimidated by life. 'We, however,' he wrote in *The Gay Science* (distinguishing his new group from those who 'chatter' in 'such bad taste . . . who have nothing else to do but drag the past a few steps further through time and who never live in the present'; those people Freud would later call neurotics),

> *want to become those we are* – human beings who are new, unique, incomparable, who give themselves laws, who create themselves. To that end we must become the best learners and discoverers of everything that is lawful and necessary in the world.

If this is excessive it may also be the kind of excess that acknowledges what it is up against – and how much people can suffer from other people's descriptions of themselves (other people's descriptions of ourselves being what culture is). So we can usefully bear in mind William James's salutary point in *Pragmatism*: 'The most violent revolutions in an individual's beliefs leave most of his old order standing'; while also taking Nietzsche's point pragmatically. Silenus's wisdom, and Schopenhauer's metaphysical contraption, Nietzsche insisted, have been perniciously misleading; but they also, as he acknowledged, freed Nietzsche to become what he called 'the great Affirmer'. We must become what Nietzsche called 'the best learners and discoverers of everything that is lawful and necessary in the world' to avoid becoming imitators rather than creators. We need to remember that when Silenus says that it would have been better not to have been born, to *be* nothing, we can take him to be saying that his demand on us is that we must agree; that he is forbidding us, by exploiting our temptation to resign ourselves, to take alternative views seriously; that, indeed, he is forbidding us from getting enjoyment from life. There may, in other words, be pleasures in life that have eluded Silenus, that he knows nothing about. And yet he is talking not only on behalf of everybody who has ever lived – on behalf of the past and the future – but on behalf of life itself (life tells us that it would be better not to have lived).

All essentialist statements – of the kind, this is what life is really like, this is what human nature is – are prone to function as prohibitions; as instructions masquerading as descriptions; as routes disguised as maps. Omniscience is always prohibitive; and prohibition always smacks of omniscience. Unlike Silenus or Schopenhauer, Nietzsche is always, explicitly or implicitly, self-ironizing. We can, fortunately, be as sceptical of Nietzsche's cultural ideals – of becoming who one is, of being self-legislating, of being masters rather than slaves – as he is of his heroes that became anti-heroes. Like Wilde and Freud, Nietzsche teaches us how to read him without the wrong kind of seriousness. Without, that is, his becoming too forbidding a presence.

II

'To be or not to be' is only the question when something about being alive has become at once unavoidable – impossible not to know – and insufferable – possibly beyond one's capacity for suffering. Or when one has been able to make one's unbearable suffering into one's paramount pleasure. What Silenus and Schopenhauer proposed cannot be, within their own terms, merely one view among others; something one might feel in a certain mood, or state of mind; or that people believe when they are suffering from depression. It is, for them – and for one part of Nietzsche – the truth from which all else follows. Not to acknowledge this would not be a blind spot, or an oversight, it would be delusional. For them it would be like a fundamental criterion; there are people who acknowledge this truth about life, people who can allow themselves to see it, and live (or not) in the light or darkness of this truth. These would be the real realists, the adults. And then there would be the others: the young, the naive, the intractable optimists, the believers in progress and satisfaction, the fabulists of redemption and enlightenment. It is clear in this story who the joke is on. Like all essentialist stories it ultimately depends on having to humiliate the disbelievers. It is not entirely surprising that one version of Nietzsche's transvaluation of all values issues in yet another version of the story about masters and slaves. So the question needs to be raised, partly to avoid the all too human, all too familiar sadomasochistic conclusions about winners and losers, the strong and the weak, the intelligent and the stupid, the knowledgeable and the naive; the question needs to be raised – because it is a recurring question – even though to be answered properly it would have to be properly historicized: is life unbearable, or have we been forbidden from enjoying it? And if life is, or is also, a forbidden pleasure, who has forbidden it, and why? And we need to bear in mind, in thinking about these questions, Deleuze and Guattari's salutary point in *Anti-Oedipus* that 'the law prohibits something that is perfectly fictitious in the order of desire or of the "instincts", so as to persuade its subjects that they had the intention corresponding to this fiction'. The law simulates and stimulates false desires, desires created by rendering them illicit. The law creates a desire for what it forbids; it suggests an interest by prohibiting it. And by the same token prevents our thinking about what may be pleasurable but unforbidden; the pleasures, for example, of what is bearable, and more than bearable. If life, or something about life, has been made, in some sense, into a forbidden pleasure, we need to be able to talk about how the act of forbidding intrigues us and distracts us.

It is, in a sense, Nietzsche – not Silenus, or Schopenhauer – who leads us to the question of whether we have also been forbidden from enjoying life; or to what extent, in what ways, we may have been forbidden from enjoying life; forbidden, not least, by cultural ideals that make the enjoyment of life well-nigh impossible. How we have been distracted from what Emerson called in his essay 'Fate' (1860), building 'altars to the Beautiful Necessity', because we have been seduced by false necessities, by spurious essentialisms. And Freud, among others, follows up on this in his psychoanalytic apprehensions. If, for example, it was a cultural ideal and not a supposedly natural predisposition – a cultural instruction, as it were – that we should marry our mothers and murder our fathers, we might think that someone was setting us up to fail. That someone was making our lives untenable through offering us impossible choices. The perennial question of whether it would have been better not to have been born at least lets us wonder about the difference between the raw and the cooked, the material and what we make of it. Whether we are making it unbearable, and if so how (for Hamlet, say, his parents have made his life unbearable, in his view, and so have made life unbearable)? It is a question that is asked when discontent is at the end of its tether; like a tantrum it bespeaks an accumulation of frustrations. It is the product of a circumstance and a moment, and their history. But it is not a question that inevitably inspires a politics; it is rather the question that is left once despair about politics, despair about what people can do for each other, has set in.

Silenus's wisdom, like Schopenhauer's, is above all a rejection of sociability, of a confidence in what people can do for each other with a view to making their lives worth living. This may feel like a stark choice: revolution or life as unbearable (you may not be interested in politics, Trotsky said, but politics is interested in you: but what interest does politics have in you once you believe it would be better not to have been born, to be nothing?). The question of whether it would have been better not to have been born, is a way of acknowledging, when it is asked, that life can seem so unbearably painful that an unintelligible alternative is suggested; a solution proposed that is always already too late. Not, it should be noted, that it would be preferable to be dead, but that it would have been better not to have been born. Not even that it is better to have had the opportunity, the chance, to come to one's own conclusions about it, about being alive; but that it would have been far better not to have been precipitated into this at all. That the question is not worth an answer and in that sense is not a question at all. That it really isn't, and so hasn't ever been, worth it. That the pleasures do not offset the suffering. That we did not ask to be born – it was not our desire, it was not one of our demands – and that we have realized that we would have preferred not to have been. The question – whether it would have been better not to have been born – invites us to think, in other words, about the pleasure of pleasure. Of what it is about pleasure, or the absence of pain, that might make it seem sufficient. Of whether, and in what sense, pleasure works, is holding us in life, keeping us going – even if it works, as Freud says on several occasions, as a bribe. And if it is a kind of bribe, how do we experience our lives, or life itself, if bribery is required?

And then, of course, there is the question of what has to happen to pleasure – what we can do to pleasure – that stops it working; of whether, as Freud suggested, there is a part of ourselves, called a Death Instinct, that hates life and wants to put a stop to it; and that is in some kind of mythic life-and-death struggle with the part of ourselves that loves life and can't get enough of it. The implication being that we – or at least the modern people that Freud was describing – are the animals that need, in some sense, to be persuaded, to be convinced, that life is worth living. That we are always tempted, as Freud says in *Beyond the Pleasure Principle* (1920), by inertia, by insentience. That it doesn't, as we say, come naturally, this belief that our lives are worth or more than worth living. For us, life is not a self-evident good. So as the only animals that, at least sometimes, seek and give reasons for being alive, who need to justify life to ourselves, we can't help but wonder what kind of pleasure reasons, and indeed justifications, are. When we are telling or are being told stories about what matters in life, it is assumed that life itself matters, that life itself is of a value that makes all other values of value. So as a preliminary to this discussion we need to bear in mind a famous remark of Wilde's. Having listened to Wilde, over dinner, hold forth in his characteristically provocative way about morality, one of the other diners asked impatiently, 'But, Mr Wilde, don't you think morality is important?' To which Wilde replied, 'Yes, but I don't think importance is.' What would be important if life wasn't? And if life wasn't important what would importance be?

The idea that it would have been better not to have been born presents the future as without promise, and the past before the past as desirable. The unknowing and the unknowable is preferred to the apparently all too known. Not the pleasure of there being no pain and no pleasure, and not the desire for more pleasure than pain, but release from all the pleasure–pain calculations, the appropriately phrased nineteenth-century 'hedonistic calculus'. It is the ultimate wish: the wish not to be done with pleasure and pain, but for the pleasure and pain never to have begun. More ambitious, in some ways, than suicide or a death wish, the desire not to have been born is the desire to have been exempted from all such considerations. It spells the futility of all the questions, all the preoccupations, all the desires, that being alive presents. But only in retrospect, when such a state can only be imagined; and you have to be alive, of course, to imagine it. The precondition for wanting never to have been born is to have been born. It is not a wish for an end before the beginning, but a wish for the abolition of beginnings and endings. It is the imagining of no imagining, a release from the need to be released from anything. Instead of the so-called perfectibility of man – the sense that there can be better future versions of ourselves, more just societies, more equable economic conditions, the hope in anticipation – it promotes the irrelevance of all ameliorative projects. As though every wish, except the wish to have never started wishing, were a fundamental misrecognition of what life was really like.

So it is also important to note that, to ask the question, whether it would have been better not to have been born, is to have already become, wittingly or unwittingly, an essentialist; or at least to have been tempted by the consolations of essentialism – to become someone who knows, or believes that they know, what life is really like. It is an omniscient position; the position, that is to say, that tragedy exposes as wildly destructive. The person who believes – however absurd such a belief can sound – that it would have been (it is a question of tenses) better not to have been born, cannot, by definition, believe in multiple perspectives, alternative views, or competing aspects. An essentialist is someone who has limited his options by always knowing where he is starting from. 'The idea that we are all strangers to each other,' Adrian Poole writes in a review of A. C. Bradley's *Shakespearean Tragedy*, 'is no more nor less of a fiction than the idea that we can reach fair understandings.' The idea that life and the world contain no true satisfaction, or that it would have been better not to have been born, is no more nor less of a fiction than the idea that we can reach other, less dispiriting, descriptions. Because Silenus cannot believe in change for the better he is an essentialist about time, for time is the medium of the endlessly unbearable. He has become the emperor of one idea. But he is also, by definition, even if only in his own mind, the person who has had the wrong parents. If they had really loved him they would never have conceived him, given birth to him, lured him into life. Good parents wouldn't bring their children to unbearable life. And if they have, they must be sadists, they must be monsters: evil monsters, or naive monsters, or both. Before psychoanalysis, as it were, personalized the issue, this was the stuff of theology.

So it isn't odd to wonder whether being alive is a pleasure and what kind of pleasure it is – for oneself, at any given moment, but also for others, for one's contemporaries, as well as previous generations. Nor indeed to ask whether life is sufficiently pleasurable; pleasurable enough to be going on with, or just something to endure with adequate anaesthetics. But if we were to ask, more abstractly, and more absurdly, whether being alive itself was, or had become, a forbidden or an unforbidden pleasure – a question that Nietzsche was clearly puzzled by – we would have to ask the confounding question: forbidden by whom? Our Creator? Our parents? And, if so, why would God or our parents create creatures that they had forbidden from enjoying their lives? What kind of god, or goddess, what kind of father or mother, would do that? Only a torturer, surely, or someone with an enigmatic sense of the good. And what kind of creatures would we be if we were the progeny of that project, of those figures? These questions – which have a long theological history – are worth broaching because no young child wonders whether it would have been better not to have been born. The question itself, one could say, is a developmental achievement. Indeed, it tends to be in adolescence that versions of this question begin to occur. That is to say, with the emergence of sexuality. It seems worth saying that if it would have been better not to have been born it is also true that everyone has been born only because two people have had sex. It is, in other words, at least from a psychoanalytic point of view, a question about, and a questioning of, both the parents and sexuality. Is sex worth it? Are the consequences of sex worth having, or living with? Clearly, there could be no naturalistic answer to this question because life as organic process neither makes us nor sponsors us in the ordinary sense in which we use those words; it can neither forbid nor unforbid pleasure. It, life, doesn't care whether we are enjoying ourselves or not; only deities or people can do that; the forbidden and the unforbidden require agents – agents who know the difference between right and wrong, the acceptable and the unacceptable, good and evil. Agents are people for whom pleasure and pain organize intention. People who forbid some things to protect supposedly better things; and for whom the better things are of ultimate, indeed legitimating, value.

As Nietzsche knew, the question of whether a life unsanctioned by a creation myth, or a genealogy – a story about why having and living and suffering and even reproducing a life was a necessary pleasure – was worth living, was pleasurable enough to be worth the suffering, was up for grabs. If it would have been better not to have been born, survival and reproduction, like all our other so-called aims and ends and values, mean nothing. Silenus's wisdom solves all the problems of philosophy. Silenus stops Darwin in his tracks; from Schopenhauer's point of view, Darwin is beside the point (why survive and reproduce if no true satisfaction is forthcoming?). Nietzsche leaves us, really, with only one question, which combines the two traditional questions. 'What makes a good life?' and 'Is it worth it?' become 'Is a good life worth it, whatever our criteria for what makes a life good?' What can we come up with, what descriptions, if any, can we create that would make the problem Silenus sees in life disappear? Or allow us to see it, as Silenus could never in his own terms see it, as simply one view among many? Could we, for example, have it both ways and realize that it would have been better not to have been born, and enjoy having been born, at the same time perhaps? What would our enjoyment then consist of? Not mastery, then, but the pleasure of what Empson called 'straddling the contradictions'? Yet we can't get round the challenge, or easily resist the nihilism, that Nietzsche, through Silenus and Schopenhauer, can't get round either, and presents us with: if our lives, our selves, our societies, were to be as good as we can make them, would it be worth it, would it be enough? Is life – even the apparently perfect life of the ancient Greeks – worth the suffering, the contingencies and determinisms and choices we are heir to? A life that can be better may never be good enough, may never give us true satisfaction. We may want more from life, more from ourselves and other people, than can be given. And it may be impossible for us to want less. We may be moral perfectionists, or what Stanley Cavell in *Cities of Words* calls 'Emersonian perfectionists', because this question, of what living without what we want turns us into, and whether we can bear this, is unsettlable; as is what, if anything, we can do about it. 'What I call Emersonian perfectionism,' Cavell writes,

> I understand to propose that one's quarrel with the world need not be settled, nor cynically set aside as unsettlable. It is a condition in which you can at once want the world and want it to change – even change it, as the apple changes the earth, though we say the apple falls. (Nietzsche's word for the spreading inability to want the world is nihilism.)

Cynicism and nihilism are the temptations, the false solutions, that what Cavell calls 'Emersonian perfectionism' can invite, the inner superiorities that can seem preferable to the conflict described. How not to fall into cynicism, nihilism, and the inner superiority that these provide, and what vulnerabilities will one be exposed to if one resists these particular unfortunate falls? These are Cavell's fears and misgivings about resisting Silenus's wisdom. Cavell's apple reminds us that moral perfectionism has unpredictable consequences; unpredictable consequences being what you get if you shrug off your cynicism and your nihilism. 'Our sense of an unattained self is not an

escape,' Cavell notes, intimating that the self is consti-
tuted partly by its unattained self, or selves, but mindful
of the perpetually ironic fact that it is our aspirations
that so often humiliate us by our falling short. And that if
our cultural ideals diminish us they are indeed strange
fictions. It is as though at this moment – and we partly
sense this through his allusion to Nietzsche's nihilism –
we should imagine that Cavell is wondering here, that if
the self-cures for Silenus's wisdom are Hamlet or Dionysus, cynicism or nihilism, what are the self-cures for
Emersonian perfectionism? Both self-cures, we should
note, by proposing a solution, are proposing that there is
one. Both, in promoting, respectively, less life and more
life, want us urgently to absent ourselves from where we
are now. And both, though apparently opposed, make an
impossible demand; or rather, ask us to want something,
paradoxically, that we can't know much about. Silenus
says, what you really want is not to have been born: Emerson says, what you really want is your as yet unattained
self. It would be part of our hope to believe there is a difference. And it might also be part of our hope to wonder
what they are forbidding us by urging us not to want to
have been born, or urging on us a better, a preferable,
future.

What then are the preconditions, for any given person,

for going on wanting the world, in Cavell's words? And what kind of life, and what kind of ideals, might sustain going on living in the world but not wanting it? And this, I think, is where Samuel Beckett's *Endgame* (1957) comes in. Not least because, as Hamm so winningly says, 'You're on earth, there's no cure for that!' And, as Cavell adds, 'No cure for that, but perhaps there is something else for it.'

III

In October 1935 Beckett went to a lecture by Carl Jung at the Institute of Psychological Medicine in London. Jung presented a case of a disturbed young woman in a way that seems to have struck Beckett. As Geoffrey Thomson, the friend Beckett went with to the lecture, described it: 'Jung had rather a dramatic, impressive way of speaking – he paused, and then said, "Of course, the truth of the matter is, this young girl had never really been born"' (Anthony Cronin, *Samuel Beckett: The Last Modernist*). Twenty years later, in Beckett's radio play *All That Fall* (1957), Mrs Rooney describes 'a little girl, very strange and unhappy in her ways'. What she calls 'one of these new mind doctors' could find nothing wrong with her . . . The only thing wrong with her as far as he could see was that she was dying . . . it was just something he said, and the way he said it that have haunted me ever since . . . When he had done with the little girl he stood there motionless for some time . . . Then he suddenly raised his head and explained, as if he had had a revelation. 'The trouble with her was that she had never really been born!'

Biographers, of course, have speculated about what this might have meant to Beckett ('There is no doubt,' Cronin writes, in the way biographers can, 'that he thought that the diagnosis was a profoundly suggestive illumination of his own case.') What there is rather less doubt about is that something about Jung's description allowed Beckett to go on thinking about something that recurred in his writing. What could it mean, that this girl, that anybody, could not have really been born? To have not been born as one should have been: with, say, the wherewithal to live. Or whatever being really born is imagined to involve. Presumably if someone feels they have never really been born, or someone describes someone else in this way, it suggests that at least someone knows, or has an idea about, what it is to be really born; what those who have been really born can do that the others can't. At its most minimal, in the way Jung and Mrs Rooney report it, it is preferable to have been really born, even though that also still leaves you really dying. There is, then, the desire not to have been born, and the desire to have been really born: born properly. And the sense that Beckett may or may not have had, that the desire not to have been born could be the consequence of not having really been born. That being the promising version.

Either way, having really been born or not, there is still the question that Cavell (and not only Cavell) sees Beckett's *Endgame* as raising: 'Man is the animal,' Cavell writes, 'for whom to be or not to be is the question: its resolution therefore must have the form of an answer . . . Why do men stay alive in the face of the preponderance of pain over pleasure, of meaninglessness over sense?' 'Ah the old questions, the old answers, there's nothing like them!' Hamm says after asking Clov whether he remembers his father; and it is remembering his father that brings on Hamlet's infamous question. An endgame is a game played with a view to ending the game, something of course that happens whether or not one does this intentionally. And finding a way of ending, or enduring – or enduring by being preoccupied about ending – what one now wishes had never begun links *Hamlet* and *Endgame* as Cavell suggests. Indeed, *Endgame* shows just how sustaining a conversation about ending can be. And also, of course, brings back Silenus. 'The very best thing,' Silenus says, 'is utterly beyond your reach: not to have been born, not to *be*, to be *nothing*.' Clov says to Hamm, 'Better than nothing! Is it possible?' 'The end,' Clov says, 'is terrific!' At the end of the play nothing has actually ended but the play.

Endgame dramatizes a way of life that is inspired by the wish not to be, to be nothing. But it does so in the full knowledge that, as Clov remarks, 'We too were bonny – once. It's a rare thing not to have been bonny – once.' Whether we begin bonny, or not really born, we are torn; and in this play, which Beckett described in a letter to Alan Schneider as, 'rather difficult and elliptical, mostly depending on the power of the text to claw, more inhuman than *Godot*', it is the ellipsis – the 'leaving out', the 'falling short', the 'failing', in the words of the *OED* – that claws at us. 'To claw', in the great dictionary of Samuel Johnson, about whom Beckett once wanted to write a play, is also 'to flatter' (to which Johnson adds, with a Beckettian flourish, 'an obsolete sense'). It can be flattering to have a sense of an ending without having to end it. It can be flattering to enjoy the words about, or to make enjoyable words out of, the predicament. 'Do you believe in the life to come?' Clov asks; 'Mine was always that,' Hamm replies. It's no life, the life to come. But there's a lot of life in saying it.

What is left out of the play are good reasons to want to have been born, really born or not. And this may be why Beckett refers to *Endgame* here as more inhuman than *Godot* (1953). It is as if to say, once you take waiting out of the picture – and Beckett refers to the play here as *Godot*, without the waiting – what is there? What is left? What are we doing once we are no longer waiting for something better, for the next best thing; no longer waiting for our supposed perfectibility, for the life to come; for what Cavell calls our as yet 'unattained self', the unattained self we assume to be the ultimate unforbidden pleasure? If your life is always the life to come, it is, endlessly and not endlessly, deferred ('We are all saved for death,' Seneca, a writer that interested Beckett, said in *Natural Questions*). *Endgame* is perhaps 'inhuman', for Beckett at least, because the characters cannot find a so-called human value to value, except the value of going on talking about how to bring life and the so-called values it encourages to some sort of conclusion – and with so much amusement, of whatever kind.

Clearly, it is an unforbidden pleasure to talk endlessly about the end, the end in both senses. And this is despite the fact, or because of the fact, that it is all talk, only words. 'Words, he says he knows they are words,' Beckett wrote in *The Unnamable* (1953); 'But how can he know, who has never heard anything else? True.'

Coda

Those who want to change us are those who want to persuade us that we have got our pleasures wrong; that what we enjoy and the ways we enjoy are in some way harmful to ourselves and others. The so-called fundamentalists, of any faith, want to settle these questions once and for all – these questions about what we should enjoy – and believe they know how to do this. So-called liberals want to keep these questions open, and undecidable in any final way. Both these groups are telling us what the lives are that we should want, and how we should get them (and what conversations we should want, and how we should get them). And both groups define themselves by what they forbid. Their motto is: look after the forbidden, and everything else will take care of itself.

Both the fundamentalists and the liberals believe that pleasures can only be assessed, or evaluated, by the harm they do. They are both, above all, impressed by our potential to harm (and believing in our potential to harm makes us more harmful). So everything ultimately depends upon how harm is defined, and who defines it. Unforbidden pleasures, at least compared with forbidden ones, are, of course, relatively harmless (people don't tend to kill for unforbidden pleasures). Clearly we want harm and pleasure to be somehow inextricable; or rather, we have come to think of the harmful pleasures as better (passion, for example, is assumed to be profounder than affection). What we don't know is what a society organized more around unforbidden pleasures than forbidden pleasures would be like; what a society would be like that didn't start from the principle, and therefore promote the principle, that we are primarily a danger to ourselves and others. We should, that is to say, also be able to start with the simple acknowledgement that it is extraordinary how much pleasure we can get from each other's company, most of which is unforbidden. And that so much depends on our capacity or our willingness to protect our pleasure in each other; and, indeed, on how we bear the consequences of its loss, and of its recovery. That we have good reasons to fear each other shouldn't be allowed to obscure how much we can enjoy each other.

But how do you get people to change their pleasures, or stick to the pleasures that are approved? Now that we are more wary than ever about conversion experiences, what ways of changing people can we afford to value? What languages can we use to evaluate people's pleasures and to transform them, and what can we then do when language doesn't do the trick? Solving these and similar questions, as Philip Larkin wrote in his poem 'Days', 'Brings the priest and the doctor / In their long coats / Running over the fields.' If it was not the priest and the doctor, who could it be now? And what might they be wearing?

Acknowledgements

Much of this book was originally presented in different versions as lectures at the William Alanson White Institute (New York), the University of Buffalo, King's College London and the University of York. I am very grateful to Jean Petrucelli, Tim Dean, David Russell and my colleagues at York, respectively, for arranging these invitations, and for making them so conducive. Hugh Haughton's introductions to my lectures in York have been a continual source. A different version of 'Against Self-Criticism' was given as a *LRB* Winter Lecture at the British Museum and was published in the *London Review of Books*. Conversations with Lisa Appignanesi, Leo Bersani, Mat Bevis, Norma Clarke, Brian Cummings, Ziad Elmarsafy, Kit Fan, John Forrester, John Gray, Stephen Greenblatt, Hugh Haughton, Michael Neve, Chris Oakley, David Russell, Ramie Targoff and Barbara Taylor have been essential. And I have learned often more than I realize from Geoffrey Weaver's Reading Group.

My editor, Simon Prosser, has been crucial in the writing of this – and indeed of all the other books I have been fortunate enough to publish with him. I have also been very fortunate again in having the book copy-edited by Sarah Coward. My agents (and friends) Felicity Rubenstein and Amy Rennert have consistently backed my writing with so much energy and enthusiasm that I almost take it for granted, but it has made all the difference.